CHAMPION MINDSET

CHAMPION MINDSET

How to Coach Yourself to Win

PATRICK MOURATOGLOU

WORKMAN PUBLISHING | NEW YORK

Copyright © 2025 by Patrick Mouratoglou

Hachette Book Group supports the right to free expression and the value of copyright. The purpose of copyright is to encourage writers and artists to produce the creative works that enrich our culture.

The scanning, uploading, and distribution of this book without permission is a theft of the author's intellectual property. If you would like permission to use material from the book (other than for review purposes), please contact permissions@hbgusa.com. Thank you for your support of the author's rights.

Workman
Workman Publishing
Hachette Book Group, Inc.
1290 Avenue of the Americas
New York, NY 10104
workman.com

Workman is an imprint of Workman Publishing, a division of Hachette Book Group, Inc. The Workman name and logo are registered trademarks of Hachette Book Group, Inc.

Design by Suet Chong
Cover photo by Menelik Puryear

The publisher is not responsible for websites (or their content) that are not owned by the publisher.

Workman books may be purchased in bulk for business, educational, or promotional use. For information, please contact your local bookseller or the Hachette Book Group Special Markets Department at special.markets@hbgusa.com.

Library of Congress Cataloging-in-Publication Data is available.

ISBNs: 978-1-5235-2787-8 (hardcover); 978-1-5235-2789-2 (ebook)

First Edition May 2025

Printed in the United States on responsibly sourced paper.

10 9 8 7 6 5 4 3 2 1

Dedication tk

CONTENTS

FOREWORD **by TK** — 000

INTRODUCTION: **What's Stopping You?** — 000

1: **Success Starts with Self-Esteem** — 000

2: **The Confidence to do Great Things** — 000

3: **Live in the Progress Zone** — 000

4: **Know the Rules of the Game** — 000

5: **Adopt a Learning Mindset** — 000

6: **Take Responsibility for Results** — 000

7: **Learn to Communicate** — 000

8: **Manage Your Emotions** — 000

9: **Your Entourage Matters** — 000

10: **Make Your Motivation** — 000

CONCLUSION: **Follow the Game Plan** — 000

FOREWORD

TK

CHAMPION MINDSET

INTRODUCTION

What's Stopping You?

When I was twenty-six years old, something changed inside me. It wasn't a sudden change; rather, it was something I had been actively working at since I was an adolescent. I left behind the anxious child I had been and became the man I was always meant to be, overflowing with a tremendous sense of purpose and a feeling of confident joy. Doubts and fears would certainly trouble me in the years to come, but at the moment I felt neither. I knew what I wanted to do with my life; I knew what I *had* to do. I felt alive, or at least more alive and surer of myself than I had ever been. Of all the victories I would win in the coming years—building my tennis academy into the largest in Europe, becoming a coach, coaching my players up to Grand Slams—this victory, a victory over *myself*, has proven to be the greatest.

Of all the defeats and setbacks I would endure over those same years, none would compare to the misery and hopelessness I had experienced as a child and teenager. Because if I hadn't won the battle inside me—a battle for my happiness, my purpose, my reason for being—then I wouldn't have won anything else.

What inspired this transformation in my twenty-six-year-old self? I'll get to that in a moment.

Let's first talk about why *you* are here: You want to win. You're sick of losing; you're tired of procrastinating; you're over being afraid; you're done with rationalizing your defeats. Even if you've never thought of your personal and professional successes and failures as victories or defeats before, I want you to start thinking of them that way now. After all, you're reading a book by a tennis coach who is judged on whether his players win or lose on the court. You play on a different court, because you're playing a different game. But these are mere details. What matters is that you step onto your court of choice with confidence, purpose, and the belief that you will walk away victorious.

> Man's greatest victory is over oneself.
> **PLATO**

In the tennis world, I am known as the "Mentalist," a nickname that accurately describes my approach to coaching players. No matter who I'm coaching, and no matter who my player is up against, my purpose as a coach is the same: to mentally prepare my player to focus on their goals and execute the game plan throughout the entirety of the match. Sounds simple, right? Except preparing our minds to face the challenges of our day and achieve the goals we have set for ourselves is perhaps one of the hardest things in life. It was hard for me when I was a child and adolescent and continues to be even today; it is hard for my players, no matter if they've won ten Grand Slams or never played in a major tournament; and it is hard for you, regardless of the challenges life throws at you or the goals you have set.

Put plainly: The greatest obstacle you will face in your life is in your own mind. Seemingly at every turn, your mind tries to sabotage your progress. Why? The mind is designed to keep you safe, and it does this by convincing you to avoid failure. Conversely, the greatest weapon you have against life's challenges is also your mind, when it is properly prepared and attuned to work for you and your goals, not against you. The chasm between these two contradictory mindsets is the difference between a life lived comfortably but without success and one that thrives on overcoming obstacles and accomplishing goals.

What I offer in the pages that follow is a program to gradually transform your mindset from being your greatest handicap to being your greatest asset. If followed correctly, this program will condition you to achieve a state of performance excellence at all times. For this is the *champion mindset*: an unshakeable belief in your own abilities matched with an unwavering focus on accomplishing your goals, not for every match, not even for every game, *but for every point*. A champion, regardless of the circumstances or details—a challenging opponent, rotten weather, an aggravating injury, loss or pain in their personal lives—performs at their highest standard at all times.

They perform at their highest standard at all times. Don't gloss over those last three words: *at all times*. They are the most important. Nearly anyone can muster the strength and courage for one heroic feat of personal achievement in their life. Good for them, but can they do it *again*? Can they maintain that competitive fire throughout the years, through defeats, through despair, through tragedies? Someone with a champion mindset can. To be more blunt, they *must*, for it is the only way to smash every goal they set for themself.

Not long ago I was talking with a friend of mine who is an

Olympic champion. After the pleasantries, he asked if I would be his coach. This request wasn't particularly noteworthy. I'm a professional tennis coach whose players have won Grand Slam titles. My academy in France is the largest in Europe and attracts the most promising players from all over the world. I'm asked to be someone's coach a dozen times a year. Coaching is what I do, and I do it very well.

Except that my friend is not a tennis player. He is an Olympic champion in a different sport. (To protect his identity, I won't divulge which sport, but it has nothing to do with tennis on a technical level.)

I should have been surprised that this athlete would come to me, a tennis coach, for help. Except I wasn't surprised at all. I was touched. I was honored. I was thankful that my friend would put his future and his faith in my coaching. But surprised?

Not one bit.

Nor was I surprised when another friend of mine who manages a major hedge fund asked if I would be his coach—not on the court, but in business. He wanted me to coach him on how to be better at what he does.

My two friends understood, as you must, that the lessons and tactics I bring to my players apply to anyone who desires to adopt a champion mindset and perform in a state of excellence *at all times*.

Before we begin, we must discuss what you need to bring to this endeavor. First and foremost, you must have a goal that you are struggling to accomplish. The details of this goal don't matter; what matters is that you have pinpointed a spot on the distant horizon that directs your actions and decisions. It could be a physical goal, like running a marathon; a professional goal, like finishing your book or starting a business; or a personal goal, like losing weight or finding a partner. Whatever it is, that is the point toward which we will strive together in this book.

To better understand what I mean, let me use a goal I had for myself when I was a child. I wanted to be able to talk to kids my age just like I saw all my peers doing. That was it; that was my goal. Such a goal might sound silly to you, but for me, a painfully shy and awkward child, it was the hardest thing in the world. When I achieved that goal, I set myself another one: I would break free of my father's authority and make friends. (You have to know my father to understand just how much this goal frightened me; you will meet him in the following pages.) The point I want to emphasize is that it is by achieving our goals that we continue to move forward and improve. The goal itself is of less importance than the desire to reach it.

Second, you must have patience. I have worked with players whose lack of patience wouldn't allow them to accept gradual progress. Their hunger—a necessity for any athlete—would overpower their humility and willingness to learn. Frustration would set in, and that's when they would lose focus. It has taken me decades to understand and embrace the lessons offered in this book. While it won't take you that long to apply them to your life, you must give yourself grace and you must have patience. As I say to my players, you must be able to look at yourself with *kind eyes*, and accept that what you are attempting isn't easy and that it's OK to fail. You will see in the following chapters how unlikely it was that I achieved any of my goals at all, given where I started. Wherever your starting point lies, tomorrow you will be closer to your goal, and that's all that matters. To use an athletic analogy, you might run only one mile today, but that is one mile more than you would have run if you'd done nothing. Don't do nothing; do something, and you will see progress.

Finally, you must look at the lessons to come as more than a training regimen; they are the keys for living. I have no doubt that if you apply the techniques of this book, you will achieve your goal, whatever it is. You will feel better than you've ever felt before. *You did it!* But here's the thing: You aren't done. When we have climbed one mountain, we must immediately set out to climb another, *higher* mountain. We never stop, because when we stop, we begin to lose our sense of focus, and when that goes, so does our champion mindset. Believe me, sometimes you will want to stop, especially after a defeat. As it is in tennis, so it is in life: The bigger the loss, the harder it is to go back out there the next day. All that work, all that discipline, all the self-sacrifice, *again*? Such an attitude has ended the careers of many great players. Even the best must lose sometimes, but that doesn't make them losers. They would be losers if they gave up after defeat. No, the best wake up the day after losing and hit the court. *That*, in many ways, is the ultimate victory.

The question, of course, is whether a tennis coach, even one who has coached the very best in the world, can turn his lessons on the court into a universal program that *anyone* can follow. Having never met you, can I still reach you—as I aim to reach all my players—in a deeply personal way and help you build a champion mindset? It's a fair question.

Coaching, when done well, begins with a bond between player and coach—a privileged connection through which the coach can perceive the player's goals, desires, doubts, and all those pesky emotions that bubble to the surface as the player steps onto the court. Through this connection, the coach will help a player mobilize the resources they need to produce a successful outcome.

The lessons I bring to my players are the very lessons I put myself through. They worked for me, and they have worked for many of the top tennis players in the world.

I am confident that they will work for you as well.

There's just one problem: I'm here and you're there. I cannot coach you in the traditional sense. I would never attempt to coach a player solely through the written word. It's not possible, because so much of my coaching philosophy hinges on my ability to build that personal connection. That is why this book is about you coaching yourself. *You* must do it. *You* must be me, in a sense, as you learn the following lessons and apply them to your life. What I'm asking of you is to be your own coach *and* player.

Does that sound hard? It is, but here's why I know you can do it: because *I did it*.

Sometimes, when I'm alone, I think about the boy I once was. Scrawny, frail, sickly, and stupid—or so I thought. I went through most of my childhood like this, with very few points of light to keep me going. I had zero self-confidence; I had no friends, since contact with strangers petrified me; I was ill most of the time; I suffered from night terrors; and I was abused at school by teachers and bullies. At home, my parents loved me dearly, but they were unable to help me overcome my problems. My father, a self-made entrepreneur, had little patience for excuses and couldn't understand why I struggled where he had excelled. Caught between school and home, I had no place to go for comfort or affirmation . . . except the tennis court, but that's another story.

No one could have imagined, least of all me, that this child would one day coach the best tennis players in the world, helping many to achieve their dreams on the biggest stages in the sport. At the same time, no one could have imagined that this same child would, by his early forties, achieve all the goals he had set for himself and beyond. Or that, having achieved them, he would be hungry to achieve even more.

Yet that is what happened. How? Well, I didn't give myself a choice. While I was never truly suicidal, I was deeply depressed and thoughts of death haunted me. By my teen years, I realized that I had to do something. If I didn't, I wasn't going to make it much longer. There was no one I could turn to, so I turned to myself. Without knowing I was doing it, I coached myself. Using the keys that you will find in this book, I adapted and honed my way of thinking to become *the* driver of my success. I gradually evolved my state of mind. I tore it down, I shook it up, and I rebuilt it—just as I sometimes do with my players.

By adopting the right mindset and attitude and by taking action, I was able to pull myself out of a vicious cycle of bad thinking, a phenomenon that captures so many who simply cannot realize their own potential. Bad thinking leads to bad habits, and bad habits lead to worse results. Those terrible results then lead to bad thinking and the cycle repeats itself. It is incredibly hard to pull oneself out of this vicious cycle.

Anxious to escape this trap, I progressively modified my perception of myself. I went from someone who had no self-esteem, someone who actively hated himself, to someone with a little bit of self-esteem. That little bit was enough to give me the power to make a change. It was a small change, but like the pebble that starts an avalanche, it was the beginning of a new life for me. I saw my qualities for the first time. More importantly, I saw that I *mattered*. This is what broke the cycle. I finally took control of my life, and over the course of ten years, from age sixteen to twenty-six, I built a new me. When I reached twenty-six, I was ready to start winning.

But if that's all I had done, then I would have fallen right back into the vicious cycle. I had to act. By putting one foot in front of the other, I actively sought to accomplish my goals. The victories started to come, slowly at first, but then with greater speed as I grew more confident and sure of myself. I made plenty of mistakes along the way, but I kept moving forward. I'd achieve one goal only to set another one. I knew that if I ever stopped moving, that would be it for me. That sickly, timid boy would return, and all I had achieved would be cast aside, nothing more than memories of a life that had once given itself a chance.

And then I experienced something truly magical. The more I accomplished, the more I wanted to accomplish. Each victory fueled my desire to achieve more. My ambition expanded; my goals kept getting bigger and grander. Even defeats, which might easily send a person back into the vicious cycle, didn't faze me. I learned from them, and then I walked right over them. In time, I was able to identify what I now call the "virtuous cycle"—put simply, when we are self-assured and confident in our abilities, we are more determined to obtain our goals. When we obtain our goals, our confidence and self-assurance increase, causing us to seek out new challenges. We aim higher because we now realize that the purpose of life isn't to achieve one goal; it's to live life as if it is our greatest masterpiece. There is no final goal; there is only the happiness, success, and fulfillment we find along the way.

Looking back on my own life as well as on my coaching experience, I've identified ten *keys* that have unlocked success for my players and for me. In each chapter of this book, I present one of these keys and tell you how I applied it in my life and in my coaching. I end each chapter with a list of lessons that you can use to apply the key in your own life. It is not enough to know about these keys; you *must* act and live them.

Along this journey, you will meet the boy I once was—a scared, timid, weak child who was unproductive at school. You will watch this boy grow into a young man and finally begin his life. You will follow my steps as I, an amateur to the tennis world, built my academy. When I stumble, you will cringe. When I succeed, you will smile (maybe). Most of all, I know you will be able to see a little bit of yourself in these moments. Even if you have never picked up a racket or don't know a grass court from a clay court, you will see that the journey we all must take on the road to performance excellence isn't so different after all. I present my victories as well as my defeats so that you may learn from my example. This includes the players I helped reach the top of the sport and those who didn't. The failures hurt, even decades later. But until we face and acknowledge our defeats, we can never move forward. I think you will find that in many instances, my defeats were more educational than my victories. When you reach the end, my hope is that you will have begun the journey that I began when I was twenty-six. All your life will be before you, with mountain after mountain awaiting you to place your flag firmly on their summits.

But this is all in the future. The only thing you must do now is start.

So, what's stopping you?

ONE

Success Starts with Self-Esteem

Over the course of a single school year my teacher slapped me forty-four times. I know because I counted them. Forty-five years later, I can still remember each one. Sometimes I was slapped for talking to the child sitting next to me; other times it was for not knowing the answer to a question. Whatever the cause, the physical punishment, designed (I suppose) to incentivize me to pay attention, produced the opposite. I fell further behind in my schoolwork, crippled by the agonizing fear that I was stupid and no good. Other children answered incorrectly, but they weren't slapped. Other children talked when they should have been listening, and they weren't slapped either. Why was I singled out?

Kids, like predators, can always spot the easy target. Throughout my grade-school years, I was frail, short, and painfully shy—it was like I was made to be teased and bullied. The snide remarks in the hallways between classes would eventually turn into lobs of spit, then pushes and punches outside of school. One incident remains seared in my brain:

As I was riding my bike home from school one afternoon, two punks jumped me. One of them, demanding my bike, flashed a knife in my face, saying, "This blade is hot for you." I handed over the bike and ran home in tears.

As a result of the bullying I experienced at the hands of teachers and other kids, I withdrew even further into myself. I believed their taunts. I believed that I was less than them. Over time, my shyness turned into crippling anxiety. The very thought of speaking to anyone produced in me such torrents of fear that I could rarely get a word out in front of anyone. I had zero friends. At night, my body would react violently to this mental anguish with bouts of vomiting that lasted until morning. I would cry myself to sleep, painfully aware that I had no control over any part of my life.

My home should have been my sanctuary from this abuse, a place where I could release the pressures of my school day with my family. We lived in a wonderful neighborhood, and our apartment was grand by most standards—except that my parents were ill-prepared to understand my problems, much less able to solve them. I don't say this to criticize them. They were not responsible for the ailments that plagued me as a child any more than they were responsible for what I endured at school. My father, a serious, disciplined man who immigrated to France from Greece, focused exclusively on my academic performance. About once a month, he would sit me down and lecture me on the importance of my studies. For him, my problems at school were *my* fault because I wasn't working hard enough. School had always come easily to him, a self-made man who, as a young person, had devoted himself to his studies and then, as an adult, devoted himself to his work. He was (and is) massively successful in the world of business. But instead of inspiring me, my father's success loomed like a shadow over everything I did—or, more often, failed to do. I believed from a young age that I lacked the qualities that made my father such a success.

My mother did her best. She would stay up with me during my bouts of nausea to comfort me, frantically worrying why I was sick all the time. She was unable to connect my frequent illnesses with my mental suffering. Like me, she felt helpless. For a family that seemingly had everything, no one had any answers for me. None, at least, that helped. At night, alone in my bed, the dam holding back my emotions would break, flooding my soul with waves of terror, hopelessness, and crushing shame. Then morning would come, and if I wasn't so sick that I had to miss school, I would return to the classroom and the hallways, where the teachers and my peers reminded me that I was weak and stupid, and the vicious cycle would repeat. Again and again.

I wasn't even a teenager and already I had decided that I was a failure.

The Crystal Ball of Self-Esteem

Self-esteem, properly defined, is how we value ourselves. It is also a self-fulfilling prophecy. When we believe we are bad at something, we avoid it; we don't push ourselves, and, critically, we give up easily. When we believe we are good at something, we turn our focus on it; we commit to practicing it, and we push ourselves to get better. In my own life, nowhere was this more evident than in my love for tennis. I discovered the game at the age of four when my parents took me to their club and stuck a small racket in my hand. With this new toy, I whacked the balls over a tiny net designed for children. I showed talent even then. The years went by and my love for the game only grew. Between the ages of seven and twelve, I would gorge myself on the French Open, which, being televised, was the only tennis event I could watch. In the evening, after the day's matches, I would head to the garden below our apartment and play with a plastic racket and rubber ball, just hitting it against a wall for hours. Well, it was a wall, but in my head, in my dreams, I was pulling off perfect forehands and stupendous backhands against the world's best—Björn Borg and John McEnroe especially.

As I got older, tennis became more than a sport for me. It was an oasis. On the court, I forgot all my problems. It was the only place where I acted and moved with confidence. I *knew* I was good because I could beat all the best players my age. The court was also the only place where I had friends. I would play against anyone. When I won, I was filled with joy. When I lost, I was devastated. I was dead. I would cry for hours afterward. But these tears weren't the same as the ones that plagued me after a bad day of school. This was sadness born out of self-esteem; I *knew* I could do better. I believed in myself on the court. I didn't have this feeling anywhere else in the world—and I clung fiercely to this one bit of joy and purpose. If I had been allowed, I would have spent every waking moment on the court. Playing or practicing, it didn't matter. I poured all my energy and effort into this obsession.

Many years later, when I finally stepped onto the court as a coach, I brought with me the memories of a childhood that had been defined by self-doubt and shame, which provided me with insight into understanding my players' troubles on the court.

I had known one of my first players, whom I'll call Anna, since she came to my tennis academy at the age of nine. She had great talent and was showing a lot of promise in her game, though she was still very young. By eleven, Anna was the number one player in France in her age group, due in no small part to her ultra-aggressive style. But then, over the next few years, her game declined, and she dropped precipitously in the rankings. After one particularly devastating defeat, I sat down with Anna and her father, who was also her coach. Looking at Anna, I could see she was clearly in distress. While she was upset from the defeat, she also seemed to have lost that incredible spark and energy that had made her such a fearless player. Now, I noticed, she was scared, and though no one had yet said anything, I knew that Anna's self-esteem was shattered. She no longer believed she was good enough for her dreams.

Her father got straight to the point: "I don't know what to do with her anymore. She doesn't listen to me. She is undisciplined. I leave her with you." Then he got up and walked out, leaving Anna and me in a cold silence. She began to cry.

Her father had been Anna's only coach. He had done an incredible job with her raw talent, but he seemed at a loss now that she was struggling to get over the next competitive hurdle. Sitting there, hearing her father-coach, and watching Anna closely, it was clear to me that he was part of the problem. He dearly loved her, but he was unable to assign any blame to himself for her struggles because then he would have to accept that he couldn't help her. By putting all the blame on Anna, he was contributing to his daughter's anxiety and shame. Coaches who blame players will never get the best out of them; good coaches blame themselves for failing to find solutions to help a defeated player. Anna had lost more than her self-esteem; she had lost her serenity.

I took over Anna's career then and there.

"Anna," I said, looking straight at her, "let's meet on the court at nine tomorrow morning."

My immediate goal for Anna was simple: bring back her self-esteem by restoring her love for the game. Her string of defeats, combined with her father's criticisms, had drained Anna of her passion. Tennis had become a grueling chore for her, as it would be for anyone who didn't believe they were good enough to compete. The reason players suffer through the long training sessions is because they know they belong among the elite. Anna needed to remember that about herself.

Other coaches might have started by trying to "correct" Anna's technical skills. But when someone is struggling with self-esteem, focusing on their mistakes will only depress them further. My task this early in our relationship was to reignite her self-esteem and help her believe she belonged on the court. I knew that Anna loved hitting the ball hard. It brought her such pleasure to whack that ball as hard as she could. So, after doing some quick technical work to improve her racket skill, I would just feed her balls that she could hit, all the while complimenting her power.

When we're stuck in a moment of low self-esteem, the best way to dig ourselves out is through the enjoyment of simple pleasures. With Anna, I went back to basics. I learned what she had first loved about tennis—hitting the ball hard—and focused on that aspect. In effect, I was telling her: *See? You're so good at it.* I didn't put any pressure on her by criticizing her; I didn't send her immediately into matches that tested her ability. My sole focus was to remind this talented teenager that she was once a little girl who just loved hitting the ball hard. In a similar way, when you find yourself at a low point in your life, go back to the simple joy that first fueled you. Don't complicate it! Strip away everything *except* the most basic element of your passion. Work on that element, again and again.

For Anna, focusing almost exclusively on what she loved worked. Rather quickly, her smile came back. In between practice sessions, I didn't overwhelm her with tennis talk. Instead, I took an interest in her life outside tennis. I wanted her to see me as a trusted friend, someone in whom she could express her true self: her fears, her frustrations, her joys, and her regrets. I could tell that part of her low self-esteem originated with the social isolation she had felt while training with her father. The moment a player begins to bear the brunt of their coach's frustration, that player will retreat inside their head. They won't express their true feelings lest they upset the coach. The special bond between player and coach is then broken: The coach can no longer reach the player, and the player begins to hide from the coach. This is what happened with Anna and her father. As the defeats mounted and her father's frustration grew, Anna had withdrawn mentally and emotionally.

To avoid this same predicament, I made a point of sending Anna long text messages at the end of every day. In these messages, I would thank her for everything she had achieved so far. I would commend her for the growth she was showing in her game, and I would express my gratitude for being able to work with her. It doesn't take much to boost a person's self-esteem. In Anna's case, my purpose with these messages was also to show her that she wasn't in this alone. I was with her, every step of the way. I would share in her struggles, in her defeats, and in her growth. We were a team.

I still had a long way to go with Anna, but by pursuing these simple steps to rebuild her self-esteem, we had established a firm foundation on which we could begin the next phase of her growth.

Belief Makes Champions

Belief is just the beginning. When our self-esteem is high, when we truly believe we will get a positive outcome, we then work with purpose, focus, and enthusiasm. Self-esteem drives our determination.

I met Holger Rune when he came to my academy at the age of thirteen. For those first few years, the young Dane worked with members of my team, but he and I didn't start working together until he was nineteen. Entering the 2022 season, Holger was ranked around No. 100 in the ATP (Association of Tennis Professionals) rankings. He jumped to No. 30 after winning a tournament in Munich but then dropped seven straight first-round matches that summer. He was at the end of this difficult stretch when he asked me to coach him. At the time, I officially was coaching Simona Halep, but she unfortunately had been suspended over a positive drug test (more on that later). The suspension allowed me to work with Holger and try to get him out of his slump.

I knew I could help Holger, but it would take some time to right the ship. Holger, whose best and worst trait is his impatience, wasn't having it.

"I want to win the next three major tournaments," he said. "By the end of that I should be in the top ten."

I could have laughed in his face. I certainly admired the young man's confidence and was happy to see that his string of defeats hadn't dented his self-esteem, but tennis success hinges on momentum—the drive and enthusiasm you take from one tournament to the next—and any expert opinion would say that Holger was clearly aiming too high.

Of course, I said none of this to him. I might have thought he was unrealistic, but I love a good challenge, and Holger had just dropped a giant one at my feet. I couldn't say no.

"OK," I replied. "Let's get going."

Over the next three tournaments that fall, Holger reached the finals in all three and won two of them. During the Paris Masters in November, Holger defeated five top-ten players in a row, setting a record. He then set another when he defeated Novak Djokovic in the final, becoming the youngest player to win the tournament since Boris Becker in 1986. After Paris, Holger was ranked in the top ten, having won fifteen of his past sixteen matches.

When one witnesses a run like that, it is very difficult to remain cynical. The focus that Holger put into his training during his incredible run of tournament finals was made possible only because he believed he could attain his goal. What makes it even more astounding is that Holger had every reason to question his own game.

But the defeats didn't lower Holger's self-esteem; they raised his focus. And this is why self-esteem forms the foundation for success. We don't achieve our goals simply by believing we can. We achieve them because our belief makes us focus on the task at hand. We will never work hard for something if we don't have faith in ourselves.

Finding That One Thing

In a childhood mostly bereft of dreaming, tennis became my big dream. On the court, I was a different child. I was confident and passionate, and I played to win every time. I never felt as if I didn't belong on the court. On the court, I could unleash my anger and frustration and show the world—or at least my opponent—that I was somebody, that I *mattered*. On the court, my paralyzing shyness disappeared. On the court, my sickly, frail body would outlast those of my opponents.

Through tennis, I was able to overcome, if only for a short time, all my physical and mental deficiencies. Though my mind struggled with schoolwork, it was able to look at a tennis court and *see* the geometry of the game. Tennis is math, after all, where angles, position, speed, momentum, and gravity all play their part in the stunning symphony of the game.

Even if I didn't know it at such a young age, I had found my "one thing"—the passion of my life, the source of whatever self-esteem I possessed. No one slapped me on the court. No one spit on me on the court. On the court, I was feared. On the court, for the first time, *I believed in myself.* I had self-esteem.

I am fortunate to work in an industry and with players who have found their own "one thing." All of us share a passion for tennis. All of us want to reach the top of the profession at some point in our careers. We have all given ourselves wholly to our craft.

As we begin this journey in which you are your own coach, your first step is to start building your self-esteem. How? By identifying your "one thing."

All your life, you have known that this "one thing" has the ability to draw from you your absolute best. No matter what others have said—parents, friends, teachers, colleagues, bosses—you understand that nothing elicits a greater degree of sheer passion than this "one thing." Your "one thing" doesn't have to be your purpose or vocation, nor does it need to be your "only thing." Indeed, you might be just starting out in life, in which case this exercise can be as simple as finding an activity in which you excel that helps you build your self-esteem. I'm talking about returning (or finding) that one thing that brings you genuine joy and elicits your best effort. By practicing it, whatever "it" is, you will build your self-esteem. You will build faith in yourself. As a child, I found solace and joy in whacking a rubber ball against the garden wall with my tiny plastic racket. Anna rediscovered joy in doing much the same. Today, as an adult, I still do it—the racket is bigger and the wall is now an opponent, but I still receive the same solace and joy. I know, without a shadow of a doubt, that *this one thing I can do*.

In any case, all I'm asking you to do is think about your passion. Write it down; stare out the window and daydream about the joy you had in doing it. As a child, before bed, I remember thinking about all the great shots I had made that day. I remember how such a simple act of dreaming made me feel so good. I want you to *feel* that fire in your belly; I want you to get excited. We are so conditioned to be "realistic" that the minute we start to daydream, a little voice whispers, "Stop being so childish." Tell that voice to go away. Remember, we're not doing anything other than *thinking* about your one thing. Besides, people who succeeded never listened to all of those who told them they will never make it.

I'm asking you to do this little exercise for one reason: because it feels good to think about your one thing. It builds your self-esteem when you imagine what you *can* be doing. It also is therapeutic to lose yourself in a momentary daydream about living your passion. You can never go back to your child self, the one for whom the whole world was wide open. That child didn't know shame or self-doubt. That child worked tirelessly to master specific goals: walking, talking, thinking. When that child failed, the child didn't even know it. That child simply tried again. Thinking about your one thing is the closest you can get to that childlike mentality of endless possibilities and limitless perseverance.

Along these lines, there is another technique I want you to try. At the end of our practice days, I would send Anna a text message describing all the things she had done well that day. I kept these little notes 100 percent positive. Even if she had a terrible day, I avoided any criticism. The reason is that we need to reprogram our brains to stop dwelling on the negative and focus on the positive. As I tell my players, never watch the full replay of a match that day; just watch the highlights. Why? Because feeling good about our performance is so much more helpful than feeling bad. Yes, defeats can be educational. But nothing is more important for our long-term performance than a high level of self-esteem.

So, at the end of your day, whether you're in bed or winding down at night, go through your day and think about all the things you did right. If your brain is anything like mine, then this exercise takes some effort. By that, I mean that it's much easier to think about all the ways in which you failed in a day. Trust me, I get it. We gloss over the good stuff and go straight to the bad. Don't be stingy with the praise. It might seem silly to feel good about how you said "thank you" to the waiter at lunch, but you're going to have to trust me here. Our purpose is to turn our vicious cycles into virtuous cycles. To do that, we need to start loving ourselves a little bit more than we have been. As Serena Williams always said to me: "You have to be your biggest supporter." Nothing is too small or trivial for this exercise. Lay it all out! It might help to write these good things down if you're a visual learner. Just seeing all the good things you accomplished in your day can be quite the mood changer. It also should motivate you to do *more* good things. Because here's a promise: You *will* feel better about yourself after performing this little exercise. Focus on your victories, forget the defeats.

Take Control of Your Life

By the time I was thirteen, I could see that my nightly anxiety attacks and my fragile health were eating away at my life. Nearly every night, my body would react to the insults and criticisms I had received during the day with violent vomiting, sometimes up to ten times a night. I didn't know how to stop it. Worse, I was slipping into a state of depression, far deeper and darker than I could have imagined. Even today, forty years later, I am haunted by those feelings of hopelessness. At the time, I understood that if I continued to accept my powerlessness, then I would never recover. I had to do *something*.

At night, I began to visualize my successes that day. I started to get the *feel* of victory. Maybe I wasn't as bad as I thought. Maybe I was actually good at some things. I accepted, without reservation, the things I did right. They were *mine*. *My* victories. One day, after yet another night of vomiting, I decided—with my whole mind and body—that it had to stop. I vowed then and there that I would never let it happen again. Strangely enough, it worked. I will add that I can provide no medical explanation for why it worked. Looking back four decades later, I think it's clear that I suffered from debilitating anxiety attacks that led to the vomiting. By training my mind to think about my victories that day, instead of my defeats, I gradually lessened the severity of the attacks, until they stopped altogether.

Regardless of why it worked, the point is that for the first time in my life, I had exerted control over myself. For the first time, I had decided my path forward. I had broken this daily cycle of defeats *on my own*. I suddenly understood with growing clarity that I had far more power over my body and mind than I had ever imagined. My mind, which had been the main antagonist in my life so far, had suddenly and for the first time become my greatest ally. I had won my first great victory. To this day, I regard that moment as one of the greatest of my life. I still had a long journey ahead of me, but I had at last finally started down the path that would lead me to my dreams.

> I am the master of my fate:
> I am the captain of my soul.
>
> WILLIAM ERNEST HENLEY

Self-esteem allows you to take control of your life. We can choose to be battered by the whims of fate, tossed from one moment to the next without any agency, ... or you can refuse to be the plaything of chance. You can refuse to be the victim and decide to become the protagonist of your story. All it takes, at first, is a little bit of faith in your own power. By believing in yourself, by deciding that you *matter*, you can steer the course of your life in the direction you choose.

Start small. Pick a piece of your life that you feel powerless to control and exert yourself upon it. With that first victory behind you, your growing self-esteem will easily overcome other insecurities and doubts that have plagued you. But it begins with one victory.

KEY 1:

Success Starts with Self-Esteem

LESSON 1:
Identify your "one thing": Spend time visualizing what it would feel like to pursue your passion.
This exercise will help clear away any doubts and shame and bring you back to feeling pleasure about the thing you love and are good at.

LESSON 2:
Visualize your success: At the end of your day, go through all the things you did right.
Watch your daily "highlight reel" before bed each night. Start building your confidence.

LESSON 3:
Reduce your passion to its essential elements: What is it that draws you to this passion?
For Anna, it was hitting the tennis ball *hard*. Remind yourself why you find joy in your passion. Start small and don't complicate this process. By keeping it simple, you will rediscover your smile.

LESSON 4:
Exert your will on yourself: Take control of your life by exerting your power on one thing that is holding you back.
By overcoming even just one obstacle, you will realize that you don't have to be the victim of fate—that, in fact, you have the power to change your life.

TWO

The Confidence to Do Great Things

When I was fifteen, my parents took tennis away from me. Or, more accurately, they told me that I had to put my studies first—that I had to get all my schoolwork done before I could spend any time on tennis. Maybe that sounds like a fair trade, but to me it was devastating. In reality, my parents' dictum meant I didn't have any time for training and certainly couldn't play in tournaments. Never one to do something halfway, I concluded that if I couldn't devote my teenage years to practicing tennis, then I wouldn't do it at all. It was a very adolescent decision, but then, I'm the same way even today— either I give 100 percent or I give nothing.

The absence of the sport I loved left a gaping hole in my life. I needed to fill it with something. In my misery, I decided that I had to do what I saw most of my peers doing: I had to make friends. Although I had overcome my nightly nausea, I was still painfully shy. The very notion of approaching a stranger and starting a conversation filled me with tremendous fear, probably because I thought that they would see how uninteresting and pathetic I was. And yet I saw the kids around me acting like, well, kids. They were goofing around; they were teasing each other; they were flirting with each other—and all these normal adolescent behaviors utterly terrified me.

I had never before been able to build any kind of social life. But in my despair, I began to daydream about being the kind of person who had lots of friends, who was surrounded by girls, who was popular and admired by his peers. I wanted to be a confident young man who was unafraid of teenage challenges. I made the decision to change my fate. After all, life is too short to be lived in fear. I asked my mom what I could do to solve my fear and my shyness. She suggested that I see a therapist.

"You mean, someone I have to . . . *talk to*?"

The thought of it was terrifying!

Nevertheless, I took her advice and found a therapist. Therapy, however, is a slow process. If I was going to overcome my fear of others, I had to act on my own. And slowly but surely, I pushed myself. Little by little. One step at a time.

I approached this new phase of my life with the same devotion I had given tennis. I *would* make friends. I faced the many fears I had about social interactions and threw myself headlong into this new struggle. In the process, I attracted (and was attracted to) the sort of kids who felt like outsiders. The rebels of the class, so to speak. Looking back, it makes perfect sense that these would be the kind of friends that an awkward kid like me would make. Like attracts like. But I didn't care. At last I had made friends, some of whom would prove to be lifelong friends.

Then came one of the most defining moments of my life.

I had proved to myself that I had the power to take control of my body and stop my nightly vomiting. Now, I was going to use that same power to take control of my life. It was 9:30 p.m. and my family had just finished dinner. I had told my new friends I would meet them at a party later that evening. All that stood in my way was an authoritarian father whose decisions were never challenged. Once the plates were cleared away, I mustered the courage and said: "I'm going out tonight."

My father's reply was instant: "No, I don't think so."

I had anticipated my father's refusal. In fact, I had memorized the words I would say in return. I knew that if I tried to argue with him I would lose. This wasn't a moment to be persuasive. I had to be decisive. I had to act.

I sighed heavily and dove in. "You see that door at the end of the corridor?" I said. "I'm going to get up from this sofa, I'm going to walk toward that door, I'm going to open it, and I'm going to go out. If you want to prevent me from doing that, then that's up to you, but if I were you, I wouldn't." Looking back, I think I was saying these words as much to myself as to my father. By explaining what I was going to do, how I would *act*, I was talking myself into it.

Silence greeted my defiant declaration. A moment passed. Maybe two. Then I got up and walked out the door. My father never moved or said a word.

Some might look at that kid who walked out that door as ungrateful for disobeying his father. I think there is some truth to this, although I believe that it is healthy and natural (necessary even) for children to test their parents' limits. I also know that this moment changed my life for the better, no less so than the moment I chose to stop being sick all the time. It was a victory, one of many that would result from my defiance.

The boy I had been a year earlier would never have had the confidence to walk out that door. Yes, I was afraid of my father, but I had been more afraid of talking to my peers. I would have welcomed my father's refusal because it would have given me an excuse to avoid my real fear.

Instead, I chose to walk out that door. I had built up my

confidence to the point that I was ready to face my fear and remove its power over me. Walking out gave me faith that I could control my life, make my own decisions, and face my authoritarian parents.

Confidence Understood

I want to make a distinction between self-esteem and confidence. The two concepts are very much related, like two sides of the same coin. They exist to complement each other. High self-esteem gives you confidence to face your fears; facing your fears makes you feel better about yourself and raises your self-esteem. It is a virtuous cycle that continues to build on itself.

Self-esteem is the belief in your own worth—the belief that something about you has real value. But knowing your own worth means little without action. There are plenty of people who have high self-esteem and yet don't ever act. Why? Because doing so might prove that they aren't as good as they believe. That would shatter their self-esteem. And for that reason, they avoid action.

Confidence is self-esteem *in action*. If self-esteem gets you onto the court, then confidence is playing with the skill, ability, and ferocity you know you possess. If self-esteem allows you to start your own business, then confidence is quitting your current job to devote all your energies and passion to that business. Self-esteem is the setup; confidence is the follow-through. Without self-esteem, there is no confidence. Without confidence, there is no action.

So that's the first thing we must understand about confidence: It is the force that creates action. The second thing to understand is that no one needs confidence unless they are afraid. Sure, you likely have great confidence in tasks that are easy for you. You know you can do them, so you don't think twice about it. But that's not the kind of confidence I mean. I'm talking about the kind of confidence you need to do the things that scare the shit out of you.

When confronted with our fears, some of us freeze. At the first sign of setback or failure, we begin to fold. In those moments, a voice in our heads whispers: *You can't do it. To take one more step is hopeless. To dig in and keep working is just stupid.* And we believe it! We avoid action because we lack the confidence to face our fears.

I have seen this countless times with tennis players—both those I have coached and those I have just observed and studied. They step onto the court with the desire and will to win ... *until something that scares them happens*. When fear—not confidence—guides your actions, you cannot play, work, or live as you are meant to. A player misses a shot—"See," says the fear, "you can't play from behind." They double-fault on a serve—"See," says the fear, "you've lost your nerve." They lose the first set in straight games—"See," says the fear, "you will never beat a No. 1 seed." Then comes the collapse. Fear has stolen their confidence.

In a tennis match (and in real life), the only real opponent is not the person standing on the other side of the court but yourself. And that is the magic of this sport: There is no chance to beat the opponent if you haven't been able to face yourself and truly win.

As a coach, it is heartbreaking to see a player fall apart. When this happens to one of my players, I accept the blame for their loss. *I* didn't prepare them to overcome those triggers. *I* failed to identify the player's fear to help them play through it. *I* misread my player's mental and emotional state before the match. But I can't blame myself when this happens to you. Instead, you're going to have to know how to work through your triggers, how to prepare yourself for the fights ahead, and how to keep pushing even when you're losing.

Fear is normal. It will always exist, especially in things that are worth doing. The bigger your desire, the bigger your fear. The bigger your fear, the more confidence you will need to overcome it. And that's what confidence is: the wellspring from which you draw your courage to face down your fear, to walk into the ring and go toe-to-toe with it. You might lose. But the next time you face your fear, you will know that its power over you is waning. Facing your fear is already a victory, and victories tend to beget more victories. Victory over yourself builds both confidence and the courage you'll need for the next fight. To embark on a journey to live a life of performance excellence is to willingly face your biggest fears with courage, and to overcome them.

What Are You Afraid Of?

What is stopping you from taking that next step toward your goals? What keeps you in a state of perpetual dreaming, never allowing yourself to convert into a state of *doing*? You might think it's some outside force, like money or time or responsibilities. It's safer and easier to blame outside forces. Safer because it means you will never have to pit your self-esteem against a true challenge and risk finding that you come up short. Easier because these outside forces are beyond your control, so it's not *you* who is holding you back; it's just the circumstances. But those are all excuses. This is the fear giving you an excuse to not act. The real reason you are stuck dreaming is that you are *afraid* of action.

That's not easy to accept, is it? It damages your ego. Good.

You've spent far too much time protecting your fragile ego from anything that might hurt it. Here's the truth: No one who lives a life of performance excellence does so with their ego intact. The sooner you are prepared to admit that *you* are holding yourself back, the sooner you can start to build confidence to overcome those fears that you don't want to admit having. True confidence requires humility.

However, before you can confront your fear, you must first understand it. Many people don't even realize they're afraid. They will blame everything else before they turn inward and dig deep to uncover that sinister force holding them back. No one enjoys identifying their fears. It's an uncomfortable process that requires deep introspection and courage. The things you uncover when you dig deep were hidden from you for a reason: to save your own ego and self-esteem. To admit to yourself that you are afraid exposes your self-esteem to the harsh light of reality. It requires admitting that you have used excuses to save your ego. These are extremely hard realizations to accept. Most people never accept them. They protect themselves in the armor of excuses because they're afraid of what they'll learn about themselves.

I said there would be work involved in coaching yourself, and now we come to the first great test. Before you can start to build the confidence to fight your fear, you first must name your fear. You must identify that part inside of you that is holding you back. Cast out the excuses! They are only mirages. Behind the facade of excuses lies your fear.

In many cases, your fear is a *learned* behavior. There was a time when you didn't have this fear, but whether from continued failure or reluctance to do something new and challenging, you created this fear inside you. I see this often with players. An athlete who plays fearlessly has a match turn against them. After experiencing a few matches like this, they begin to develop a fear of it happening again. Before, this player wouldn't have let a setback like a bad match affect their performance. But now, the player conditions themself to respond to this fear in a specific (and destructive) way, holding back when a match begins to go badly. With enough repetition, sometimes over the course of years, their destructive response to fear becomes as second nature as their fearlessness once was.

Extracting yourself from this dangerous trap requires clear thinking to identify *what* you are doing and understand *why* you are doing it. Most people aren't cut out for such painful introspection. Why? Because it takes brutal honesty. The person we lie to the most is ourself. Faced with a challenge, we lie to avoid it. Faced with ambition, we lie to stay put. Faced with opportunity and joy and fulfillment, we lie to forget them.

No more lying. Look inside yourself and search for the fear that dwells in the darkness. This is the fear that suddenly strikes the day after you embark on something worthwhile. It is the fear that keeps you from doing what you were born to do. It is the fear that grips you right at the moment when you decide to take the harder path. Most of the decisions you make in life—about yourself or others—are affected primarily by fear. It's not the hope of doing or not doing; it's the fear of doing or not doing. Apart from love, fear is the strongest of human emotions—and the most elusive. It will convince you that it doesn't exist.

Let's look at some common fears that might be holding you back.

Fear of failure. This is a common one for many, but it's also a misconception, in my opinion. It's not fear of failure that stops us; it's the fear of suffering that comes from failing. I'm not referring to physical pain; I'm talking about shame. We would do almost anything to avoid feeling shame, including lying, cheating, or stealing. Have you ever held back from total commitment to a project for fear of failing and, therefore, suffering? Failure is less painful when it does not involve intense effort because we can always keep in the back of our mind the idea that, if we had really committed, we might have succeeded. But if we truly try and still fail, then we have no one and nothing to blame but ourselves. This is one of the greatest lies we tell ourselves. All of us have acted on it at one point or another, and none of us felt better afterward. For a moment we learn the truth: that giving our all and failing hurts much less than the shame of giving up.

Fear of the unknown. The older we get, the more we become locked in our ways. When we are younger, there is a window of opportunity when exploration and adventure excite us. We know we can get by on very little, and so money hasn't sunk its vicious fangs into us yet. We haven't yet put down roots with work and family, so we are drawn to distant horizons, both literally and figuratively. And yet part of the human experience is the creeping rigidity that makes us settle down and build walls around what is ours. We become far too comfortable in our own little bubbles—our home bubbles, our work bubbles, our social bubbles. We'd rather exist in the life we know than go in search of the life we want.

Fear of success. Yes, some of us are terrified about achieving our dreams. It makes no sense! How could we be afraid of achieving our dreams? Because it's not so much success itself that terrifies us; it's the consequences of achieving it. Sometimes we're afraid that we won't have earned our success. This is what's known as imposter syndrome. Simply put, we are afraid that we don't really have what it takes, we got to the top by dumb luck, and any day now our colleagues, our friends, and our family are going to figure out that we don't deserve their esteem. At other times, we are afraid that once we have achieved something great, we will have to repeat the performance again and again. The very thought exhausts us, so we choose to take the easier road. I see this kind of fear often with players. They know that however much they might struggle and sacrifice to rise in the rankings, that effort would be nothing compared to what they will have to go through to defend their top rank. Fearing the high expectations of others doesn't just steal confidence; as I have seen as a coach, fear of success can end a player's career.

I can't possibly know the fears that exist deep within you and keep you from living a life of performance excellence. I do, however, know that they're there. Now, it's your job to find them.

The Fear of Pressure

One of the most pervasive fears is the fear of pressure. When the stakes are high, many us wilt under the enormity of the goal we are trying to achieve. The pressure can be so high that it becomes debilitating. We simply cease to function. Yet if we want to live a life of performance excellence, we must accept and learn to appreciate living with pressure—and we must acknowledge that the pressure will grow as we rise. Anything worth doing or achieving comes with pressure. If we want to succeed, we *cannot* avoid pressure and the stress it can cause.

But as with any fear, the key to handling pressure is confidence. Pressure exists for a reason. Think back to when you were in school and you had a big exam coming up. The pressure was immense. If you used that pressure to study harder, then when the day of the exam came, you might still have been nervous, but you also felt ready. This simple example explains how we can minimize the stress that pressure can create. You knew you had prepared for the exam by studying hard, and so you had confidence that you could succeed. Pressure focused your energies and attention on the task at hand. *That's* the importance of pressure. Deadlines, exams, matches, meetings, that first date—whatever is creating the pressure, when we harness it to our preparation, we succeed.

Preparation builds confidence, which reduces stress. Because it's not the pressure that is debilitating, it's the stress that the pressure creates. Much like the confidence-fear balance, confidence and stress are also in balance. When one increases, the other decreases. The key to reducing stress is to increase confidence. We are not in control of the pressure we face; it will exist regardless of what we do. It's how we use that pressure that defines the outcome and decides whether we create more confidence or more stress.

When we understand something, we remove its power to scare us. Fear is greatest when it is unknown, when our minds are free to conjure up a menacing monster. That fact is famously illustrated in Steven Spielberg's movie *Jaws*, in which the audience doesn't see the killer shark until one hour and twenty minutes into a two-hour movie. But that's what makes that first two-thirds of the movie so terrifying: Our imaginations build something that is much scarier than whatever the filmmakers could have created. Once we see the shark, the movie enters its third act, in which the protagonists attempt to kill it.

Many years ago, an Olympic champion swimmer explained to me her very unusual method of handling the stress that can grip an athlete who has made a mistake. I've seen it often enough on the tennis court: A player's single mistake can destroy all their confidence. In her case, she explained that, at all the swim meets leading up to the Olympics, she would in every race *deliberately* make a mistake. So, for example, at the start of a race, she would wait a second too long to dive into the pool. Or she would start too fast. In every race before the actual Olympics, she would do something wrong on purpose. Then, after making the mistake, she would go on to win each race regardless. I asked her what this unique style of training did for her.

"I mentally prepared myself for any mistake I might make in the Olympics," she said. "I then knew that if I made a mistake, I wouldn't panic, because I would have already experienced it and still won."

In other words, this swimmer removed the fear that would have come from the unknown of making a mistake. She wanted to understand better how she would perform under such conditions. I can only imagine that those first few races created a lot of stress for her! But over time, as she better understood how to respond to mistakes, she reduced her stress and built her confidence.

Confident Humility

When I see players on tour, I can usually tell which of them has a low level of confidence: They're the ones lashing out whenever they are criticized. Criticism cuts deepest for those who believe deep down that they aren't good enough. The more arrogant their attitude, the more doubtful they are of their own performance. Anger is their armor; it shields their real feelings and provides an artificial boost to their self-esteem.

Moreover, some of the least confident people I've met were those with the greatest talent. I have long believed that innate talent is one of the worst things for an athlete because it teaches them all the wrong lessons. They play and progress without much effort. From a very young age, they are told how talented they are. It quickly becomes their greatest asset, their identity, the one thing that defines them. As they grow older and the quality of their opposition becomes better, they start to protect their asset at all costs. They become scared to lose, and this fear is greater than their confidence in winning. They don't want to risk the one thing that defines them. But to excel at the highest levels of athletic competition is to risk losing. Players who define themselves not by their innate talent but by their work ethic, their competitiveness, their determination, can accept losing as part of the process of getting better. But for the naturally talented player, losing will destroy their ego; it will shatter their self-worth.

When a talented player begins to lose, they get scared. That fear will come out as anger, but don't let that fool you. It's fear. They're afraid because they feel that if they lose, then others will question their talent. They have no confidence inside them beyond a belief in the superiority of their own talent. When that goes, it's game over. Hard work and discipline would have filled out their talent with useful tools to overcome the rough parts of a match, but the talented player never bothered to find those tools.

On the opposite end of the spectrum, I can tell which players have the confidence to be champions. They're the ones listening to advice. In fact, they *want* advice or constructive criticism because they're always looking to get better. They don't bristle or lash out when someone highlights their mistakes. They listen. They have the confidence to understand that criticism isn't an indictment of their character; it's another moment to improve their game. They're the ones who are hungry to learn more. They ask questions. They ruthlessly prepare themselves, mentally and physically, for each match. They take losses hard, but they go back out because they have the confidence to know that a loss isn't the end; it's another opportunity to improve. Because they know they got to where they are through hard work—not just innate talent—they know that *more* hard work is the answer.

Indeed, there's a humility that comes with true confidence. The confident are never "too good" for something. They seek out those who will challenge them, hold them accountable, ensure that they are doing absolutely everything they can to win. Perhaps most of all, the truly confident feel blessed. They believe that the opportunity they have to live a life of performance excellence is a gift. And the worst thing one can do with a gift is squander it.

Remember, what defines champions is not their talent. Would you define Serena Williams, Novak Djokovic, or Rafael Nadal as simply "talented"? No. What defines them is their attitude, their confidence in their ability to achieve their goals, and their drive and determination.

Little Victories

Before I walked away from tennis, I used the sport as a tool to boost my confidence. I chose to play *only* against players who were weaker than me. Seems a bit unfair, doesn't it? Wouldn't I have improved my game by playing stronger opponents? The answer is yes, but there's a caveat: When you are struggling with your confidence, little victories matter. A little win against a weaker player will do more for you than a loss against a great player. I didn't realize it at the time, but I had hit upon a coaching technique that I would later use for my players whose confidence had been shaken or absolutely shattered.

Sometimes winning is the best medicine. Winning makes

us feel good. It satisfies our competitive spirit and it banishes fear. The seventeenth-century French dramatist Pierre Corneille once wrote: "To win without risk is to triumph without glory." Sounds great, except this is the worst coaching advice you can get. Easy wins may not get you glory, but they can build your esteem. If you want to win the big battles, you must be ready for them—and you won't be until you have had a lot of little victories.

Eventually you must test yourself against the best, but that comes *after* you've built a foundation of confidence. If there is one thing that I want all my readers to take away from this book, it's this: Without confidence, you will not excel. With confidence, you can do anything.

Returning to Anna, through my coaching tactics, she had rediscovered her love of the game and remembered why she was so good at it. Her smile returned. As happy as I was, especially given that I was almost brand new to coaching, I knew she still wasn't ready to compete. We had more work to do.

I had learned enough about Anna to identify her fear: She experienced every match as a terrifying ordeal that almost always ended in disappointment. When Anna made a mistake or when she lost—whenever she felt the sting of humiliation—she would fall back on bad habits, both in her attitude and in her technique. Bad coaches would try to fix her by criticizing her bad attitude and changing her play style without trying to understand the root cause of the behavior.

I understood that the bad habits were not who she was as a player; they were how she had learned to respond when a match turned against her. When Anna experienced frustration on the court, it would give way to resignation: Since she was going to lose anyway, she reasoned that it would be easier to just give up. And yet after these matches, she felt horrible shame—and there is nothing easy about shame. In losing without putting up a fight, Anna was destroying herself.

I set to work on rebuilding her confidence so she could learn how to fight. How? The same way I did as a kid: by letting her win little victories. I put her on the court with players I knew she would beat. I didn't tell her I was doing this, though, because this was a very dangerous time for Anna. She had found her desire and was ready to get back on the court, but if I thrust her suddenly into the lion's den, then she would have been eaten alive. All her fears and anxieties would have come flooding back, erasing all the work we had done together to grow her self-esteem.

No, it had to be baby steps; it had to be little victories.

In the beginning, it was important to create positive experiences to start Anna's "reprogramming." In our daily training sessions, I created game situations in which she could shine. She had grown accustomed to positioning herself too far behind the baseline—it was as if she was afraid of the court itself! So, I got her to do exercises in which she would spend time inside the court and begin to feel safe there. From the other side of the net, I would feed her balls that I knew she could whack back with all her amazing power. Instead of retreating to the baseline, Anna relearned how to rally inside the court. She relearned that her tremendous power was her best asset, and that she couldn't use it from so far back on the court.

In the afternoons, I would pit her against male opponents. I knew she wouldn't judge her performance against male players as much as she would against female players and would play less fearfully. With the pressure taken off these matches, she started to go for those amazing power shots that had once defined her game. I also put her up against inferior players, telling her I didn't mind if she lost so long as she met certain parameters, such as playing serve-and-volley at least twice in each of her service games. Against the weaker opponents, Anna started to play with confidence again. With each little victory, she added more tools to her toolbox. Slowly but steadily, we reprogrammed her play style and ended up breaking her vicious cycle.

Then it was time for her to face better male opponents. Before each match I spoke to her opponents, asking them to play normally for most of the match, but to let her win without making it obvious. Again, this might strike some as antithetical to the spirit of competitive sport. After all, tournament players wouldn't let her win! But I wasn't concerned with tournaments. I was concerned with building Anna's confidence through little victories as she tore through the ranks of male players at the academy. She progressively realized she was playing with more confidence and far less fear than she had in years. That was my point all along. If you want to build confidence, little victories are the best way to do it.

Before long, she was ready for matches against stronger female opponents. At first I set her up in matches against weaker players whom I knew she could beat. But when she faced stronger opponents, I backed away from asking them to let her win. (In truth, I chose many of these stronger opponents because they were also trying to regain their confidence. I knew that Anna had a good chance to win, and that the victory would mean a lot because she knew they were good players. The results of this "little victories" strategy were undeniable. Anna became increasingly relaxed on the court, which allowed her to be bolder and more fearless than she had ever been. Her programmed behavior of retreating to the baseline was replaced with a new behavior: stepping up into the court and hitting that ball with all the power she could muster.

It was beautiful.

When I sensed that she was ready for competition, I put

Anna in a local French tournament rather than an international one. Again, I was helping her take those little steps back into the higher levels of the sport. She was still only a teenager, so she had time to hone her game before joining the ranks of the elite players. A month before the tournament, her WTA (Women's Tennis Association) ranking was above 1,300. At the tournament, she went on to beat, in succession, two 1,000-ranked opponents, two 500-ranked opponents, one 300-ranked opponent, one 250-ranked opponent, and one 150-ranked opponent. In the end, she lost the final match against a top-hundred player, in three sets. Her defeat aside, the reprogramming was complete. She was playing with confidence; she was playing fearlessly; she was playing the best tennis of her life.

Over the next year, Anna would break into the top hundred in the world juniors rankings and into the top five hundred in the WTA, and she won the French under-sixteen championship. I was bursting with pride and told her so. I didn't say that I was surprised, however, because I wasn't. I knew she could play like that, and, finally, she did too.

Little victories lead to championships.

Live Fearlessly!

The point of building your confidence is so that you can tackle life without fear. To acquire a champion mindset, you must remove the block that is stopping you from *acting*. Why do people feel so much more confident after they've had a few drinks? You may be terrified of approaching an attractive person , but after a few drinks, you walk right up to them with confidence. We know why: The alcohol removes your fear.

Of course, drinking and drugging are temporary solutions. The confident drunk guy will be the same timid guy the next morning. You don't want to be the person who needs alcohol or drugs to overcome your fears. You want to be the person who makes their approach dead sober. *That* person is someone who goes after their goals fearlessly.

The purpose here is to help you realize the connection between confidence and action. Confidence is a conditioned behavior, just like any habit, good or bad. When we act with confidence, we tend to get good results, and even if we fail, we don't despair. Sometimes we need to have a few little victories to get us back on track, but that's all part of the virtuous cycle. Acting with confidence builds our behavior. When it works, we act with more confidence. When it fails, we either get back out there or we go back to building our confidence.

How does all this look in action? I'm fortunate enough to have worked with the absolute epitome of confidence in action. Her name is Serena Williams.

Serena, whom I coached for ten years, possesses a fiercely powerful confidence that she can achieve whatever she wants. Every time. There is the reality that we see before our eyes, and there is the reality that we construct for ourselves, which gives us a rough idea of the limits of the possible. Serena has forged her own reality, disconnected from that of most other people. She believes she can win a Grand Slam tournament while injured and sick—as she demonstrated in 2015 when she won the French Open while running a 40°C (104°F) fever. She thinks she can start training barely a few days after giving birth. She is convinced she'll hit an ace with every serve, even on second serve, and takes every possible risk to do so. It's not that Serena has no fear; rather, it's that her confidence, backed by a belief in herself, overpowers what fear she has. Her confidence cup runneth over. She never thinks about taking the excuse: sickness, pregnancy, mood, whatever. She ignores them all.

This level of intense confidence is what allows Serena to play carefree. And that quality is one of the reasons for her success. She's all action; she just *does*. That's why I always refused to give her on-court coaching during matches, not even once per set as allowed by WTA rules. I didn't want her to think that she needed me to win. Her ability to find solutions was unmatched. If she called on me for help, she would potentially lose that belief that she could turn a match around when in trouble.

There is a lot more to discuss about Serena in the chapters to come, but I felt it necessary to show readers what living fearlessly looks like. Now, I'm not saying that we all have a Serena Williams inside us. She's a once-in-a-lifetime personality. But I *am* saying that there is an explanation for her historic success on the court that has very little to do with her innate talent. Serena's father, Richard, once told her: "Don't let doubt enter your house." Serena's self-confidence allowed her to laugh in the face of fear. That's her secret. That's my secret for you. Build your confidence so that you can crush your fears. Without excuses, you have only one thing to do: act.

My Year of Silence

As I said earlier, I took my mother's advice to find a therapist, even though I doubted therapy would work. How would talking to a stranger help me overcome my fear of talking to strangers? Nevertheless, I found myself seated in front of a psychoanalyst not long afterward. I mustered up enough nerve to ask him how this whole process worked.

"It's very simple," he replied. "You are sitting in a moving train. Describe the landscape to me."

Ugh. I wanted a solution! Not this.

That first year of seeing the therapist was painful, like going to the dentist once a week. Sitting across from him, a lot of thoughts came to my mind, but I couldn't express them. I felt exactly as if I was facing someone I didn't know, with mental and verbal paralysis gripping me. And so I said nothing. *For an entire year.* Our soundless sessions felt more like mental bouts. Though I hadn't said a word, I would leave exhausted and ashamed. On my way home, I would roar in resentment. After each session, I swore I would break the cycle and say something the next session. But I never did.

Then I noticed a change within me. Little by little, I started to understand my mental block. I could not speak because I was afraid of judgment—in this case, the judgment of my therapist. What would he think of me if I finally opened my mouth? My self-esteem was so weak that I felt that everything I was thinking about was uninteresting and pointless. I realized that the reason I could not socialize in my regular life was exactly the same: fear of judgment. I had to face my fear and start. As Arthur Ashe is said to have advised: "Start where you are, use what you have, do what you can." Do not wait to feel ready; you will never feel ready enough. Just start.

After a year of therapy, I finally spoke.

I'm sure whatever I said that day was banal, but that didn't matter. I was expressing myself for the first time.

My therapist ended this triumphant session by saying, "This year of silence will be part of the story of your analysis."

I was proud of myself. I finally understood that we grow by acting, not waiting. It thus follows that we should seek out positive experiences that help reinforce and expand our confidence. Eventually, though, we must move past the little victories that support our newfound confidence. We must test ourselves against stronger opponents; we must use that confidence to push through our fear of the stronger challenge. In this way, we gradually habituate ourselves to *act* when we encounter a difficult situation. We push onward and through it. Then, we have disentangled that experience from fear; we've replaced the fear with a positive feeling.

Decision-making is like any other muscle: Every time you overcome your apprehension about leaving your comfort zone, the decision-making muscle is strengthened and will be better able to respond when the next opportunity arises. Positive action initiates a virtuous circle. The stronger your self-confidence becomes, the more likely you are to grasp opportunities to improve and grow. Eventual failure will not dent your confidence because your self-esteem is sufficiently solid to accept it and move on.

From that day when I finally spoke a word, I put faith in myself. I had recorded another victory in my match to overcome my own personal defects. Now I was hungry for more. My confidence surged. My life began to open, and my mind began to dream.

KEY 2:
Confidence Is Action

LESSON 1:
Fear is holding you back: An inability to act or follow through stems from fear.
To begin to build your confidence, you must first name your fear. Why are you afraid of pushing ahead? What is stopping you from living a life of performance excellence? Find your fear, and you will find your answer.

LESSON 2:
Win "little victories" to build confidence: Acting with confidence is a learned behavior, which is why you can start building your confidence in small but significant ways.
I call these moments "little victories," because in themselves, they are rather trivial. But each one helps your confidence grow a little more. From now on, I want you to win every day. Find little battles that you feel you can win and go for them. Each one will build your confidence, so that when you are ready for the championship, you come ready to win. The more victories you gain, the stronger you will feel and the bigger the battles you will win.

LESSON 3:
Decide to act: As the Nike slogan says: "Just do it."
You are presented with opportunities to test your decision-making skills many times a day. As with the little victories, by themselves these moments aren't very significant. But each time you decide to act, rather than avoid, ignore, or retreat, you exercise that decision-making muscle. You turn *action* into a learned behavior, a reflex, just as much as *not acting* has been a reflex. You are eager for new opportunities, you seek out new adventures, you pop the bubble of comfort and expose yourself to unpleasantness. Stop dreaming and start doing.

THREE

Live in the Progress Zone

There came a moment in my early twenties when, barricaded with my coworker in a landlord's office while an angry resident pounded on the door, I wondered if my career path had taken a wrong turn. At this point, I was working for my father, whose business owned a collection of real-estate properties, including two apartment complexes situated in the heart of Paris.

My job was to go door-to-door collecting rent from the tenants. My colleague and I quickly learned that not every tenant was happy to hand over their hard-earned money. In earlier years, while still a foolish teenager, I had substituted violence and intimidation for my lack of confidence and self-esteem. I had eventually grown out of that macho phase, but it taught me how to stand firm in the face of aggression. Still, the best thing I can say about that job is that I survived.

After a year, I "graduated" to a position with more management responsibilities, and to handle the workload I decided to set up my own agency that would take care of rent collection for the housing property. I didn't necessarily realize it at the time, but I was learning a valuable lesson for life and business: namely, do what works. I didn't have a clue what I was doing, so I just did what made sense. It worked.

Meanwhile, my father was moving into the renewable energy market—hydroelectric power stations, to be precise. I was put in charge of managing the on-site operations of stations situated all over the world: Guadeloupe, Martinique, and La Réunion. The business flourished, and a year later, I was entrusted with managing hundreds of solar power projects. Having served my time in the trenches and thrived, I could see that my father was proud of me. I had overcome my rough start in life and displayed the kind of qualities he most admired: hard work, determination, and a head for business.

The conversation with my father that I had been expecting happened when I was twenty-six. He spoke first: "You have worked in my company for six years now, and you have proved yourself. The business has grown a lot, and we have some big projects ahead. I would like you to be part of them. We can build these businesses together. You are ready to work alongside me."

My father was offering me a very promising future, especially for someone who only a few years earlier had believed himself a complete failure. Considering how enormously profitable my father's companies had become, I would have to have been a fool to walk away from it all.

But walk away I did.

Leaving the Comfort Zone

Human beings are creatures of habit. From the time we are babies, we tend to thrive in a lifestyle that emphasizes routine and familiarity. The one exception to this rule are the teenage and early-adult periods. Those are the years in which we press against the boundaries of our childhood, as we should. We are instinctively drawn to leave our parents' nest and spread our wings in the wide world. We go to college, we travel the world, we get a job in the big city, we *live life*. This period can be longer or shorter, depending on the individual, but for most of us, there comes a time when we are drawn back into a life of routine and familiarity. Think of a rocket ship that breaks free of Earth's atmosphere to explore the mysteries of the universe only to return home, pulled back by Mother Earth, where it is safe and comfortable. The fiery recklessness of our youth runs out of fuel, and we slowly but inexorably drift home. We find a spouse, we build a career, we have children, we *settle down*. Living life becomes building a life.

The tendency to settle down can contribute to the routine and discipline that are essential to making any dream come true. But sometimes this instinct goes too far. We become too comfortable. We begin to cling to our comfort like a baby its pacifier, and for the same reasons: because it soothes us and helps us cope with life's many problems. Personal, emotional, professional—it doesn't matter what kind of disturbance is breaking our zen, we have conditioned ourselves to equate that discomfort with fear. So, we avoid uncomfortable situations, even to our own detriment.

> The only person who likes change is a baby with a wet diaper.
>
> **MARK TWAIN**

I see this dynamic at work with players all the time. Athletes, probably more so than people in any other profession, aren't just creatures of habit; they are demons of *extreme* habit. If something works for them, nothing less than a planet-destroying meteor will dislodge them from their habit. Even when they start to lose, a player will cling to their old ways like an addict. Very few people can break a habit cold turkey—and even if they do, they are usually miserable doing it. The only way to break a habit is to replace it with another habit. In other words, you don't command a player to stop doing the bad habit. You subtly guide that player into a different habit. This defines much of my coaching with players, in that I work *with* them, not against them.

Your comfort zone is a set of predictable behaviors and habits that you consistently repeat, as if you're an object in space orbiting a planet. This orbit is your comfort zone. A jet-setting playboy can be just as trapped in his comfort zone as a family man is. A comfort zone is simply where we retreat to when life becomes uncomfortable.

Let's take an example:

You're going to the birthday party for one of your best friends. When it's time for the cake, one of the attendees turns to you and says, "Stand up and make a toast!" Your pulse quickens as a blush covers your face. Speaking in public, even in front of an audience of friends, is terrifying for you. You shake your head and say, "Oh, no, I'm fine." But your friend continues to encourage you to stand up and speak. In the space of a second, you have moved from a zone of comfort to one of discomfort. At this point, you would do almost anything to get back into the familiar orbit of your comfort zone.

The discomfort zone is characterized by a sudden responsibility in an area in which you have little experience or confidence (public speaking) and through which you have something to lose (your credibility, your honor, your dignity). The moment you are placed in a zone of discomfort, your brain starts to panic: "Will I be able to do this? How will people perceive it? What if I'm disappointing?" In short: "What will happen if I'm no good?" Faced with these questions, one conclusion is inescapable: "I have nothing to gain, but I have a lot to lose."

When we're back in our comfort zone, we sigh in relief: "Phew! That was close."

Staying in the comfort zone very much applied to me in my youth. But with any refusal to step outside my comfort zone came a sense of shame. It would gnaw at me for hours, sometimes days, after the incident. The instant relief of avoiding an uncomfortable situation turned to a long-term disappointment as I chided myself (yet again) for succumbing to my fear.

The Progress Zone

The first two chapters of this book deal with self-esteem and confidence because they are the building blocks of the champion mindset you need in order to move out of your comfort zone, to act differently, to step into a state of discomfort. But it's only discomfort because it's new. What you're really doing is stepping into the progress zone.

I overcame my childhood trauma and gained a self-confidence that has never left me because I learned to love the progress zone. The comfort zone is a zone of boredom, a place where nothing happens, a no-man's-land, a state of non-learning. The progress zone is a world where you overcome your fears, where you learn new skills, where you meet new people, where you confront your opinions, where you get to know yourself, and, above all, where you grow your confidence in yourself and in your ability to achieve everything you desire.

I couldn't change myself by stepping into and out of the progress zone as the mood struck me. I had to live in the progress zone, and I learned that not only could I do that, but I thrived there. I had never thrived in anything. And yet here I was, an employee of my father's company, and crushing it. What, I asked myself, had I been so afraid of all these years?

When I declined my father's offer to work beside him, it wasn't because I was scared or ungrateful or because I didn't think I could do it. The problem, as I saw it, was that his proposition would leave me in a comfort zone. Staying there offered no challenge for me, and without challenges to overcome, I would never grow. I declined my father's offer because I was ready to tap into the potential I felt burning inside me, and that potential led me in a different direction. Behind this potential was a wellspring of self-confidence, ready to spill out of me. I didn't know how, but I knew that I would succeed in whatever it was that I was about to do. In fact, I didn't know anything. But that's the beautiful thing about the progress zone. When you live in it, discomfort turns to excitement. It becomes a force, like rocket fuel, propelling you forward. Outside the love I have for my family and friends, it is the greatest energy I have ever felt.

> Later it will be too late. Our life now.
> **JACQUES PRÉVERT**

What happened to me when I was twenty-six? I was finally ready to succeed at life.

Ask yourself this question: how much do you want another life, a life where you will finally tap into your immense potential, a life in which you will work towards goals that make you dream? Would acquiring such a life be worth a little bit of discomfort? You bet your ass.

The Next Summit

At the end of 2012, Serena Williams had reclaimed her spot as the best tennis player in the world. Under my coaching, in just six months, she had won Wimbledon, two Olympic gold medals, the US Open, and the year-end Masters. Serena should have been on top of the world, but she wasn't satisfied. Happy? Yes. Content with her dominance? Absolutely. But satisfied? No. The word *satisfied* was wholly alien to Serena Williams. I could see the hunger in her eyes, and I asked what was on her mind.

"Roland-Garros," she said without hesitation, referring to the French Open. "I haven't won it in ten years. We need to find a strategy to help me win it next year."

So we did. And Serena won the 2013 French Open by defeating her rival, Maria Sharapova, in straight sets in the final. *Now* was she satisfied? Please.

Right after the trophy ceremony, she asked me to join her for her post-match recovery session. We talk about the tournament for a few minutes or so, and then she blurted out: "OK, now we have to win Wimbledon!"

Good grief. If ever there was a time to rest on your laurels, it was less than ten minutes after winning your thirty-first straight match and becoming the oldest woman ever to win the French Open, a title she had been chasing for ten years. . . . But Serena wasn't one to *ever* rest on her laurels. For her, as it is for champions, the joy isn't really in winning; the joy is in the challenge, in climbing that next mountain. That's the "juice," the motivation that keeps them on top for so long.

The moment you are satisfied with what you have or where you are, you step out of the progress zone. Indeed, it is very difficult to maintain your hunger once you've stood on the summit. You should know now that the purpose of this book isn't to help you achieve your dreams. The very notion assumes that there is an end to the journey. No. There isn't an end, because the dream isn't what you're after; what you're after is to always live in a state of performance excellence. *Always.*

This doesn't mean that you must never be happy with what you have. Happiness and satisfaction are two different things. The moment you say "I am satisfied with where I am," you will crawl back into your comfort zone. The way to stay in the progress zone is by setting goals.

The Purpose of Goals

Dreams are cheap. When dreams only live in your head, it costs you nothing to keep them there—and that's where they will stay unless you leave your comfort zone. So, how do you take your dreams and make them real?

Many of us know where we want to go, but we have no idea how to get there. Put another way, we can see the destination, but we can't see the path to reach it. Or, if we can see the path, we start to imagine the sheer amount of discipline and work it will require to follow that path and it all seems too daunting. Either way, we want to leave our comfort zone, but we don't know how.

Here's how: You leave your comfort zone by setting goals and achieving them.

Wait! Isn't *goals* just another word for *dreams*?

It certainly can be, but not in the way I'm using either word.

Dreams, properly understood, are motivations. They are the fuel that gets you going, but the dream itself isn't what you are trying to accomplish. Every tennis player wants to be a champion. That's their dream. It excites them. It makes them work hard every day. It keeps them up at night. It gets them up in the morning. The arduous hours, the sweat and the tears—they all have a purpose and that's to be a champion.

But what does it mean to "be a champion"?

For starters, it means winning tournaments.

Great! So the goal is to win tournaments?

No. How do you win tournaments?

By winning matches. So, to be a champion you have to win matches?

Nope, winning matches is just the result of winning points. To be a champion you have to win points?

Almost there. A player's goal is to focus on what they need to do on every point.

It might seem like I'm being overly pedantic with my verbiage here, so to help illustrate the point, I'll share some real goals one of my players wrote down. These were her goals for a particular match.

- **First goal: PLAY DEEP.** Every time I hit a ball, I want to push the opponent back. Why? Because I protect myself from attacks, and it potentially creates short balls that allow me to control the rally.

- **Second goal: PLAY AGGRESSIVE AND MAKE THE OPPONENT RUN.**

- **Third goal: STAY POSITIVE.** How? Play every point like a new challenge. When I miss, I stay excited and enthusiastic because I have the opportunity on the next point. Talk to myself in a way that will keep me constantly in that mindset.

As you can see, these goals are extremely precise. They must be, if the player is going to get anything out of achieving them. After the match, regardless of whether the player won or lost, our focus is to measure how they performed on their goals, which tells us exactly what to work on to improve next time.

I actively discourage my players from thinking about winning a match. Once they take their focus off every serve and put it on winning the match, they will start to lose. "Win the match" cannot be a goal. Winning is the reward for achieving your goals for the match.

It's critical that your goals should depend only on you. A goal can't be conditional on your opponent, or a competitor, or some other uncontrollable variable. A goal isn't reactive. You must be able to pursue it regardless of what your opponent does. Too many players enter a tennis match with the goal to "play well." Champions win regardless of whether they're having a good day on the court or a bad one. That's one of their greatest qualities: to be able to win on a bad day. How do they achieve that? They focus on the right goals that depend only on them, and by achieving their goals, they achieve a win.

The consistent focus on achieving a specific goal produces a habit, or, perhaps more accurately, it strengthens a muscle. When the muscle is properly conditioned, it works automatically. If a player consistently performs well on a specific goal over a series of matches, we can remove that goal from the list. But we don't rest there—now it's time to add a new goal to the list. We must always be pushing ourselves into the progress zone, into that discomfort from which we grow our skills and our confidence.

Building Your Goals

Like building blocks, your goals must build on each other over time. When you accomplish one, you push the goal posts a little bit farther down the field. You are never "done," because you can always progress further.

I can't tell you your goals. Goals are tailored to each individual through an honest assessment on what needs to be achieved in order to reach their dreams. I can, however, show you how to find them.

Take your dream or your aspiration and work backward. Just as we did in defining what it really means to be a champion, drill down, step by step, until the abstract starts to become real. Don't stay in the realm of abstraction. Go deeper. *How* can you reach your dream?

Each goal should be:

- **Dependent only on you.** The goal is achieved or remains a goal based solely on *your* actions. If achieving a goal is contingent on the actions of others or dependent on circumstances, then the goal is achievable only under certain conditions. Part of the joy of achieving goals is to realize you have the power to direct your life.

- **Perfectly controllable.** You must be able to work on your goal at any time under any conditions. You know what we call things out of our control? Excuses. If you lose focus, if you take a day off, *it's on you.*

- **Achievable.** Take the wisdom of "little victories" and apply it to your goals. Keep your goals simple and well within your reach—at least to start. Think of a non-runner training for a marathon. On Day 1, do you try to run ten miles? God no. Five? Still too high. Three? Maybe. One? Yes. One mile. Just one. One mile today is more than you ran yesterday, and *that's all that matters*. You are in the progress zone.

Goals should start small and be extremely focused. There isn't a set number of goals. If you do the exercise above and find yourself with only one goal, fine. Work on that one goal. You are out of your comfort zone. You are progressing.

You'll know when you've accomplished your goal: It will feel easy. You have slipped out of the progress zone and into the comfort zone. Now it's time to expand the goal or find a new one.

And you will find a new one. Why? Because you're going to experience the same exhilaration I did when I started to accomplish my goals. The same excitement and joy that I see in my players when they start to accomplish their goals. It's addictive. It's beautiful. You will learn how to thrive outside your comfort zone and you will want to have that feeling with you always. This joy is nothing less than the power to control your life.

This is why the dream, the thing we are trying to achieve, isn't really the point. It gives us a direction—a mark to shoot for. Absolutely have your dreams, and let those dreams guide your goals. But here's a little secret: You will find, like I did, that the juice, the joy, isn't in achieving your dream; it is in the pursuit. Savor it. Be greedy for more of it.

The Start of the Journey

When I put my tennis racket away as a teenager, I thought I was done with tennis for good. It was a naive thought, but I didn't pick it up again for seven years. In that time, I had achieved my own successes and victories over myself. I had built my self-esteem and my confidence. That I did all of this without tennis was a very good thing. It meant that my worth, my ability to perform, wasn't solely reserved for a single activity. My time in my father's company showed me that I had qualities that could serve me no matter what I chose to do with my life.

When I picked up my racket again, it was just to spend a few nights a week practicing on my own. This little taste of the sport that had once consumed me was enough to bring all the passion surging back. I felt alive. I took my training a step further and hired a coach to give me formal lessons. I even entered a few tournaments, mostly just for the pleasure of competing. I simply didn't have much time to do more than pursue tennis as a hobby.

This thought bothered me. *Did* tennis need to be just a hobby? How might I make tennis my job? I knew that it wasn't going to be as a player. I was twenty-four, and while that is young in human years, in tennis years, I was an old man. That train had left the station. But one of the reasons tennis is such a beautiful sport is that you can play well into your old age. It *is* a hobby for millions of people who never played professionally.

My coach at the time—who happened to be the only person I knew in the tennis world—shared my passion. He wasn't famous, but he had a true love for the sport. He dreamed of training more players. Well, why couldn't he? So, we started talking, and soon I had rented out two courts at a club outside Paris. I posted an advertisement in *Tennis Magazine*, and in January 1996, we welcomed our first clients. Mind you, I wasn't a coach then. My colleague was the coach, but I was the guy finding the clients and working with the club to negotiate court prices. I was taking care of the business, and he was in charge of the sports side. We found older players who simply wanted to get better and compete in some of the amateur tournaments. Within six months, we had about twenty clients. That's how my first tennis venture, the Tennis Competition Training Team, was born. I managed all this in addition to my day job working on my father's renewable energy plants.

But here's the thing: As small as it was—I mean, we didn't even have our own courts—the TCTT gave me so much joy. Using what I had learned working for my father, I had taken an idea and turned it into something real. It existed! And I had no idea what I was doing. But we don't need to have an idea to get started. In fact, sometimes "having an idea" is what keeps you in your comfort zone; you *know* how hard it will be, and so you never try. I went into my first tennis venture with the attitude of "let's see what works." When something worked, I moved on to the next goal. If it didn't work, I tried something else.

It was around this time that I began to dream, imagining my life working in the tennis world in some high capacity. Coaching was not yet a dream; rather, I wanted to build an academy that would attract the best young players in the world. I knew exactly how that sounded. It sounded conceited. It sounded arrogant. Who was I to think that I could build a world-class tennis academy? To which I would have answered: I'm nobody, but I'm smart, I have huge motivation, and when I dive into something, I learn extremely fast. I was brimming with confidence in myself and in what I could achieve. No, what I *would* achieve. Dream big, start small.

I had started the journey that would become my life. But I still had one goal that I needed to achieve, one that I had failed at years earlier as a teenager whose parents just didn't understand my passion for tennis: I had to convince my father to support me on my journey.

KEY 3:
Live in the Progress Zone

LESSON 1:
Identify your comfort zone triggers.
What activities or behaviors trigger your need to find safety in your comfort zone? What absolutely terrifies you? What habits do you have that are holding you back? Asking these questions and searching for the answers will help you identify your personal comfort zone. Then ask yourself, what is stopping you from living the life you desire? What is keeping you from taking that first step? In which area can you improve and make your life different? Introspection is never easy, so don't be too hard on yourself.

LESSON 2:
Identify your goals.
This can be a daunting task because there could be an infinite number of things you must achieve to realize your dream or potential. Sometimes, all you need to get going is to start living differently—eating healthier, exercising, reconnecting with the activities and hobbies that bring you joy. Remember, goals are achieved only by leaving your comfort zone.

LESSON 3:
Never be satisfied.
You can be content with your life, but never satisfied. Satisfaction means there is nothing left to do. You set life on autopilot and take a nap. There is a life out there that you are meant to live. Go find it!

FOUR

Know the Rules of the Game

I didn't need my father's permission to start a tennis academy, but I did need some capital to fund my dream. My parents loved me and wanted me to be happy, but they did not realize what tennis meant to me. When they told me to put down my racquet all those years ago, they had been concerned about my future. They thought that I had a weak personality and that I would be eaten alive in a world that is so competitive. For them, education was the easiest, less risky path. Their evaluation was simple: "Patrick will go to university, and then he will get a job and there won't be any reason to worry about his future."

Had I presented my case in *their* language—i.e., as a plan for my future—they likely would have been more accepting. If I had understood their concerns, their fears, I would have given myself the chance to convince them. This time the conversation would go much differently—not because my father had changed (he hadn't), but because I had. Now I was ready to give him a reason to believe in my passion and dream. I was going to talk to my father on terms that *he* could understand.

After he offered me a job working beside him, I replied: "Thank you very much for your incredible offer. But tennis is my life. I know how lucky I am to have found my passion, and now I'm ready to pursue it. I want to be able to give young players a chance that I never had. I want to grow my small tennis academy, and I can't do that if I'm also working for you. When I'm your age, I want to look back on my life and be proud of what I accomplished. Pursuing my dreams in tennis will do that."

I waited for the reply, unsure of how he would respond.

"Very well," he said, "I understand. How can I help you?"

I think that if I hadn't had an answer—a thoughtful, convincing answer—to this very simple question, then I might have left that day without my father's blessing. But I *had* come to this conversation prepared.

"I need funds for two projects," I said. "First, I want to recruit a top coach, someone whose very name would give my academy credibility and attract the best players. Second, I need financial backing for the group of talented players that I will select."

I went on to explain that these two elements would help me create a brand, one that would inspire and represent the academy's values. We would be able to attract young players because they would understand that my academy is where champions are built. Moreover, I wanted my academy to be a world leader in educating young players not just in tennis, but in all educational disciplines.

"And that is why I need investment now," I said, finishing up. "We can build a unique brand that will have a major value on the market. We will create the biggest tennis academy in the world, and then we will develop more academies around the world."

This is my father's language: passion, education, building

value, creating a global brand that represents integrity, and growing a worldwide business.

"Very good," was his response. "Draw up a business plan and we'll look at it together."

That was it. I learned several lessons from this conversation with my father, but perhaps the most important one is to understand the rules of the game. What game specifically? In my case, the "game" was convincing my father that a course of action was a prudent and potentially lucrative one. I had lost that game when I was teenager—heck, I didn't even know I was playing it! But on my second attempt, I entered the court with a clear understanding of and respect for the way my father looked at the world, and at me. After six years spent working several jobs in my father's company, I had dropped much of my childhood naivete and foolishness about the real world. I saw how ideas become reality; I saw how decisions were made; I saw how one convinced someone else. In short, I had one of the best *business* educations that exists. And my father was nothing if not a businessman. When I learned the rules that governed his world, I came ready to play—and win.

The Power of Observation

As a boy, I had a fascination with watching people interact with each other. My own incredibly debilitating shyness no doubt spurred this within me: I was intensely curious about how others were so effortlessly able to do something that caused me extreme anxiety. I wanted to know *why* they could live their lives so easily while I couldn't even speak a word. So I listened to their conversations; I observed their body language; I compared how boys talk to boys and girls talked to girls and how they talked to each other. Like Jane Goodall with her apes, I hid myself in the forest of anonymity and took notes on the behaviors of these curious creatures.

In my observations, I picked up on the tiniest details: the way people dress, an intonation of voice, a raised eyebrow, a hand gesture. Without knowing it, I was learning both verbal and nonverbal communication and what those two can tell you about a person. Everyone conveyed a message, and I was determined to discover what those messages said. I began to understand why one person could hold power over others; I saw what made some people leaders and their peers followers. By scrutinizing every detail and feature, I even came to understand how other people were feeling at a given moment. Without speaking a word to them, I knew when they were proud, upset, shocked, confident, impressed, or frightened. More importantly, I knew *why* they felt a certain way. I could often predict their reactions when they faced certain situations.

While I continued to observe on the sidelines, I was slowly learning the rules of their particular game—in this case, the game of adolescence. Most children absorb the social rules that govern the playground and school hallways without realizing it. They simply adapt their behaviors to the rules— or they don't, and they get ostracized. For me, I was quite consciously learning the rules, even if I was too afraid to play the game. In time, the powers of observation that I developed as an adolescent would prove invaluable for my adult life. I didn't need someone to tell me how they felt; I often could discover it by simple observation. I could divine another person's wants, desires, and frustrations just by spending a few moments with them. I don't listen to what people say, I *hear* what they *think*. Of all the skills I brought to coaching, this has proved to be the most powerful.

Rules Govern Everything

Every field of life and sector of work operates under a set of rules. Our success in these areas depends on how well we absorb and adapt to these rules. By understanding the rules of a specific field, we give ourselves the power to operate efficiently and effectively within it. Like an architect's blueprint, the rules reveal details and levels that might otherwise go unseen. We see why certain individuals are successful in this field and why others aren't. With clearer vision, we can identify the steps to get ahead—as well as appreciate our own strengths and weaknesses. Some rules are clearly expressed, while others are not. There are also some unofficial rules, such as those that govern what makes businesses successful, how to be persuasive, how to instill loyalty, and how to speak to people so they stand with you rather than against you. There are rules you can learn from books and rules you can learn only by being totally immersed in a particular world.

Some might read this as an argument for conformity—for the idea that you must *fit in* to succeed. That's not my meaning at all. Rather, think of a great tennis player. No matter how good they are, they must follow the rules of tennis. Everything depends on it. An amazing, unreturnable serve that faults is not an amazing serve. A dominating forehand that hits the ball outside the line is not dominating. No matter how great a player is, if they don't play by the rules, they will lose.

Consider a CEO who is brought into a company from the outside. Before the CEO can make a single decision, they must first understand the company and the industry: who makes the decisions; who defines the parameters of success or failure; who holds the purse strings; who the customers are; who the suppliers are; and on and on. Like the tennis player playing by the rules of the game, the CEO must know the basic rules of the business in order to do their job. By themselves, these rules give form and function to the particular field and provide essential knowledge for anyone who wishes to succeed within that field.

But this most basic level of rules isn't enough. Going deeper, a field's rules are also the behaviors, the culture, and the habits of the people who operate within it. We can't learn these rules by simply identifying the person in charge of operations or the regulations that govern how that field operates within the law—i.e., like the rules of tennis. Instead, we learn these rules by observing the people in the field, much like how I observed my classmates in school or how I observe my players before I coach them. Studying people is how we best learn the rules under which they live and operate.

Those who ignore the rules, or who think the rules don't apply to them, find life—and success—much harder than it needs to be. They are seen as arrogant and difficult. They repel others when they should be attracting them. They might know all the details of a company or field, but their peers don't see them as teammates. More importantly, they don't make good decisions because they lose touch with their goals.

In short, knowing the rules of the game is about preparation. And not just any preparation, although learning the nuts and bolts of any field is vital. Rather, it's a conscious attempt to understand the behaviors of those around us. Once we learn this, then we will have the ability to thrive within a given field. It's a way of approaching the world that requires a little bit of practice and a lot of patience.

When Serena Williams approached me to be her coach, I knew it was the opportunity of a lifetime. I already had a very good sense of who she was because I had followed her career closely. A few years earlier, *L'Équipe* magazine had approached me to interview Richard Williams, Serena's father and coach.

I jumped at the chance to sit down with the man who had raised and coached not one but *two* tennis superstars. We had a wonderful, illuminating conversation in which Richard discussed his philosophy on raising daughters into *confident* women for whom no doors were closed.

This interview, however, was conducted during Serena's peak performance period. Several years later, when she came to me, she wanted to return to that level of dominance but felt she needed a different coaching approach. So, as much as I thought I knew about Serena, I realized I needed to know a *lot more*. I needed to learn her rules. I did some basic preparation and research. For instance, I read her book, *My Life: Queen of the Court*, and I watched a lot of her matches and documentaries. I learned her game inside and out and I learned how she operated. I learned how she had been raised and talked to, what tennis meant to her, how she dealt with victory or defeat. I picked up on certain words she used to describe herself and her tennis. I picked up on the verbal and physical cues that revealed her emotions—excited, angry, happy or frustrated.

From her father, Richard, I learned how he got the best out of Serena and what motivated her to play her best tennis. I learned how demanding she was with herself, and how he had created a culture of victory around her. I focused on the words he used to describe her drive and her technique. I knew that to succeed in my task, I had to emulate Richard's approach. I had to talk to her as he had talked to her, I had to motivate her the way he motivated her, and I had to let her be herself, because in the end, she already knew how to be a champion. My task was to remind her of that.

When I went to the court with her for the first time, knowing how she had been taught throughout her life, I mentioned that she was not "moving up to the balls" during the practice.

She responded: "That is incredible! My father always tells me to do that!" I knew that these words would resonate with her; I knew that she would think: "I have not been winning as much in these past two years because I have not been doing what makes me great. This man sees the same things as my father. I can trust him."

Several years later, I would often tell the press how Serena was going to win this tournament or that tournament. But she was in a difficult phase at that time and under a lot of pressure. At this period of her career, she had lost her confidence; she was doubting her game. My confident (almost arrogant) attitude upset her. By predicting victory, I was setting expectations that she wasn't sure she could meet. She called me and asked me not to say those things.

"Serena," I replied, "do you remember how your father would say the same things about you back then? How you were going to destroy everyone and win every tournament?"

"Yes," she said.

"Did it bother you then?"

"No."

"Then don't let it bother you now," I said. "I'm doing the same thing he did. And I know it works well for you."

I was able to do this because I knew her rules, her language, even if she had forgotten some of them. I knew how to coach her because I knew *how* and *why* she had become one of the greatest to ever play the game. And I knew she wouldn't be happy until she was *the* greatest. My predictions weren't for the press; they were for her. It was as if I was saying to her: "Here's the bar. Now jump over it." Serena was never better than when she *had* to deliver.

There are coaches who apply the same mentality and program to every player they coach. This has never made sense to me. In fact, I think it's probably the worst way you can coach someone. Since no two people are alike, then each one has a unique set of motivations and fears, strengths and weaknesses. Trying to shoehorn everyone into your personal coaching box will lead to disastrous consequences. I wasn't going to force Serena into any kind of prefabricated program. I would listen, I would ask questions, I would observe, and *then* I would decide and act. After Serena, I worked with Simona Halep, another multiple Grand Slam winner and the No. 1 player in the world. She processed things very differently than Serena. She could not perform well under any expectations. She performed best when she felt that I did not expect any kind of results from her. Every person is unique and deserves a unique approach.

When I began coaching Aravane Rezai in 2010, she was ranked No. 60 in the world. She began to play better, rising as high as No. 40, but then she had a bad result in Rome, where she lost in the first round. All this time, I had been observing Aravane both as a player and as a person. Her loss and her behavior during that match answered some lingering questions. After the match, a French newspaper reporter asked me if I was happy with the results I had seen so far. Clearly I wasn't. Though Aravane had risen in the ranks under my coaching, I knew she could do so much more. I said as much to the reporter, but I added that up until that point, I hadn't had all the information I needed. What I meant is that I hadn't yet fully understood the rules that governed Aravane. Her loss in Rome gave me what I was missing. I told the reporter that now I had the whole puzzle. "Follow her results closely from now on," I said. "You will be surprised." A week later, Aravane won the Madrid Open Masters 1000, defeating Justine Henin in the first round and Venus Williams in the final.

Too often we make decisions based on incomplete (or faulty) information. If there are questions yet to be answered, as there were with Aravane before her loss, then we must get those answers before committing to a course of action. What this means is that until we know the rules, we must be flexible in our decision-making process. We must have the patience and the confidence to wait until we have gathered all the information we need to know before taking action.

Depending on the player, I may vary my data-finding techniques. Sometimes I withhold information or provide partial information just to see how my player responds. I use a lot of the "test and learn" process. I can tell a player how to do something, or I can simply ask them to show me how they do it. I might speak with authority in my voice, or I might let a player think my wishes were their decision.

By employing all these various tactics, I come to a deeper understanding of my player than they even have of themselves. I know their desires and their weaknesses, I know what motivates them and what scares them, I know how to get them to listen and learn, and I know just how far I can push them.

The inevitable question: When will you know if you have all the information? My reply: You will know because everything will suddenly become very clear.

Know When to Break the Rules

When I started my academy, one of the bits of advice I heard from others was that I needed to go through the French Tennis Federation, the governing body of the sport in France. Most of the smaller clubs in France were connected to the federation, which would pull the best players and coaches in each region to create a league. The federation would then take the best from the leagues to represent France at international tournaments. The relationship between the clubs and the federation is supposed to foster a nationwide network that promotes and improves the French tennis community. To that end, the federation would send experts to the local clubs to scout potential talent and report back to the federation.

It made sense that to build my own "club" I should go through the federation. After all, the federation appeared to have an iron grip on the best players and coaches in the country. So I looked into it and visited with the man in charge of the Paris league, whose attitude toward me, an unknown, can only be described as imperial. He made it clear to me in no uncertain terms that if I wanted my club to be a success, *of course* I had to work with the federation.

I walked out.

What I would come to realize is that the federation believed it owned any player who was with one of the clubs. The moment a player showed promise, the federation would move them out of the club and up the ladder. I didn't want that. My academy wasn't going to be a way station for the best players to use and then leave when they were "ready." I wanted my players to understand that my academy would train them in the best possible way to realize their potential. I didn't want to just adopt coaching methods that someone else would give to me. What if they weren't right? What if they did not work the way I expected?

Even after I had declined to join their network, the federation tried to rein me in. Some time later I vividly remember getting a call that a federation representative was on my court taking notes on my players. I rushed down there and threw him out. "If someone enters your living room without being invited, what would you do?" I said to the federation guy. "You would kick him out, right? So please get off this court!"

The dirty secret that I came to realize is that I didn't need the federation. And breaking this "rule" would bring me closer to my own goals. I knew that I could start an academy and make it a success on my own, without relying on a larger organization that would never leave me alone. In time, the federation would come to see me and my success as something it had to crush, but those days were still far off. At that moment, when I was just beginning to build my academy, I knew that I had everything I needed (except for the name—but I had a plan for that, as you'll read about in a moment).

I fell back on the business education I had received while working for my father's companies. Building something from nothing can seem like a daunting challenge, but not a mysterious one. There were rules, there were obstacles, there were prerequisites, but no mysteries. And I wasn't cowed by the goal of building *my* business. I had the confidence, built by years of experience, to know that I could do it. I set for myself daily goals, whose accomplishment would get me closer to the larger goals, which would eventually get me to the goal of owning my own academy. That fact that I was doing this in the tennis world, in which I was a stranger, was mostly (but not entirely) beside the point.

Learn Your Own Rules

When I want to do something, I pursue it to the limits of my endurance. It's just the way I am—an aspect of my personality that I discovered early on. While working at my father's company, I saw how my drive, when harnessed to clear, achievable goals, could be the secret to my success, even in a profession for which I had little passion. I knew what I needed to succeed in starting my own academy, and it would require every ounce of my ability. I was certainly nervous, and perhaps also a bit intimidated, but my excitement and enthusiasm about that project were far stronger than my fears, and so my inner machine was amped up. This is how I operate; this is one of my own rules.

To learn your own rules requires being obsessively honest about your strengths and limitations. For me, this wasn't a particularly difficult self-examination. I had known my weaknesses since I was a child, and I had identified and developed my strengths as I entered adulthood. As I contemplated my plan of action for the academy, I knew that my lack of public profile in the tennis world was a weakness. I wouldn't succeed if it was just me, Patrick Mouratoglou, on the marketing materials. No one knew who I was, and that would present quite a problem when I tried to hire the best coaches and entice the best players. I needed someone who was well-known in the tennis world to join me.

This insight might sound fairly obvious, but no one has ever accused me of being overly humble. Even then I wasn't. I had the confidence to believe I could own my own academy but the humility—and insight—to realize that I couldn't do it on my own. Understanding these rules about myself, combined with the rules that governed business endeavors as well as the tennis world, I knew I had to find someone whose name would attract money, coaches, and players. That person would be Bob Brett.

Here's one of my personal rules: I succeed when I feel pressure. My performance shines in must-win scenarios, which is why I actively create pressure for myself. When my collaboration with Serena became public, I took a lot of interviews, during the course of which I would talk about how Serena would crush the competition. Wasn't I simply setting myself up to fail? By predicting victory, I wasn't leaving myself much of an escape hatch should she lose. But that's the point. To give my best (and for Serena to give her best), I needed the pressure. I needed to know that failure wasn't an option, that failure meant extreme personal and professional humiliation in the press. Critics called me a braggart (they still do), but I'm fine with that because I know my own processes. I know what I need to succeed.

A Fateful Meeting

Near the end of the 1990s, Australian coach Bob Brett was one of the most successful tennis coaches in the world. He had taken Boris Becker to No. 1, then Goran Ivanišević to No. 2. His star was rising. When I first put my sights on Brett, he had just started working with Nicolas Kiefer (whom he would take to No. 4 in the world). As I mentioned previously, I had come to understand what I needed (and didn't need) to build my tennis academy into the best in France. I knew I could rely on myself for everything except the most important thing—a name to draw the best players and coaches in the country. No one would want to join a Mouratoglou Academy, but a Bob Brett Academy? Brett's name alone was all the marketing I would need.

A chance encounter at my local tennis shop put the wheels in motion. At the Paris store where I went to get my rackets strung, I ran into John Elliot, an Australian who happened to know Brett personally. I explained to him what I was trying to build with my academy, and that I wanted to bring in Brett as my brand name. I then asked if he could arrange a meeting with Brett for me. Elliot said he would try. A day or two later, he called to say that Brett agreed to meet with me at his hotel during the French Open. Brett had one hour to give me.

You better believe I did all I could to learn Brett's "rules." I studied his coaching style, I read and reread interviews he had given, I watched his players perform again and again. My strategy was to make Brett appreciate that I wanted *him*, not just because he was a famous name in tennis, but because he represented the values, the ethics, the style I wanted to build at my academy. On the day of the meeting, I was bursting with excitement and enthusiasm. In terms of its importance, the only thing I could compare this meeting to was the meeting I had had with my father about starting my own academy. And just like at that meeting, I wanted to speak Brett's language. I had to convince him that I—an absolute nobody in the tennis world—was the right man to join up with as partners. Looking back, it's almost comical that I went into that meeting as confident as I was. Other than a plan and a dream, I had nothing. No infrastructure, no financial guarantees. But I had done my homework. I could decipher what a man like Brett, at the top of his game but also nearing middle age, would want to leave as his legacy. That's what I was going to offer him: a chance to leave a legacy.

I met Brett at his hotel. I had an hour to convince him to join me. I needed only ten minutes. Within moments of our first handshake, I knew I was speaking his language by the way he smiled and got animated at my offer, as if he was imagining the possibilities already. When the hour was over, he stood up, shook my hand again, and said: "I'm with you, Patrick. Let's meet again after Wimbledon. Prepare the contract and I'll sign it then."

When the deal was done, I thought about the boy I had been, the man I had become, and the long, twisting journey that connected the two. There wasn't much left of that boy in the man . . . except a passion for the sport of tennis. That passion was now a career, and I was about to embark on another journey.

KEY 4:
Know the Rules of the Game

LESSON 1:
Prepare and observe.
In any game, athletic or not, you must prepare yourself wholly before deciding to play. That means learning the rules. Some rules are easy to identify, while others—those that deal with the behavior of people—require patience and observation. Enjoy the discovery and know that the knowledge you gain will boost your confidence when you step onto the court.

LESSON 2:
Know when to break the rules.
It is not always to your benefit to follow the rules of a particular industry or profession. If the rules don't make much sense for you and your goals, break the rules. But remember that breaking the rules requires that you know them in the first place.

LESSON 3:
Know your own rules.
You, like everyone else, have your own set of rules that affect your performance. To perform at your best, you must create conditions in which your qualities and talents can shine. When you work alongside others, be forthright about how you work at your best, while also acknowledging and accommodating how your coworkers work at their best.

FIVE

Adopt a Learning Mindset

As a student, I was thrown out of three educational establishments for insolence and academic incompetence. By my later teenage years, when I should've been preparing for university, I was spending my evenings hanging out with drug dealers and punks, crashing parties and starting fights, while my parents waited worriedly for me to return home. Education, knowledge, curiosity, my future—these were the last things I cared about. My world was one of alcohol and violence, late nights and women. As is typical for a teenager, I believed I knew everything that was important to know. If I didn't know it, it was not worth knowing.

Looking back, I now see my willful ignorance as one of the consequences of my education. Teachers had pegged me as "no good" from an early age, and eventually I believed them. I turned my back on school and pursued an empty, hedonistic lifestyle, where bravado and fists—not grades and studying—proved one's worth.

Things started to change when I turned nineteen. I was two years behind schedule in taking my "A-level" exams, which is the equivalent of earning a high-school diploma in the United States. Unwilling to give up on their son, my parents put me in a new school called the Institut du Marais in Paris. I went reluctantly, having long since accepted what every other teacher had said to my face, and almost immediately was greeted with a learning experience that shattered my expectations.

One moment in that first year of my new school stands out. My parents had accompanied me to a meeting with the director of the school to discuss my performance. The director had witnessed the same thing that teachers had witnessed all my short life: I was not unable to focus during class; I was mentally in my world and dreams. Though he made the same observation as everyone else had through all these years, he came to a totally different conclusion. The director explained to my parents that I "had an artist's mind, a creative mind." He continued: "Patrick might learn differently than other students, but he's no less capable. He'll do something creative, trust me." Never in my life had I heard an educator praise me. What others saw as a weakness, he saw as a strength. The power of being *seen*—well, it is unbelievable! At the same time, it is interesting to see that the same observation can lead to such different conclusions. This is the difference between someone who looks at you with a kind eye and someone who looks at you with a judgmental mindset. Was he right? Was I capable? Was I smart? *Could* I excel at school and in life? I wanted to know the answers to these questions. But the only way I could find the answers was to start learning. And for the first time, thanks to the way this man was considering me—and that is the right word; I felt consideration—I found the motivation to learn.

It might not sound like a big moment, but for me it was the start of a transformation. Or, more accurately, it was the first crack in my carefully constructed dam of ignorance.

All it took was *one* person to believe in me. Where my previous teachers had seen daydreaming stupidity, this one saw unrealized talent—a spark that I had never known existed inside me. The actor Gérard Depardieu, in his autobiography, describes a similar moment he had with a psychiatrist during one of his stints in jail as a teenager. The psychiatrist looked at his hands and said that the young Gérard had "sculptor's hands." Depardieu writes:

> I'm still a child, and this guy sees in me an artist. It probably means I'm better than a thief. . . . That day I learned I am an artist. With all my strength I wanted to believe it.
>
> This is the immense beauty of life: that a single encounter could bring you so much more than 10 years sitting on the bench in the school classroom repeating stupidly what a professor says.
>
> This man who refuses to see all the shit around me stops his eyes on my hands and pronounces these few words, sets me free, and open all the doors to me.

I felt the same. I wanted to believe that this director's assessment of my "creative mind" was true. Suddenly, I wanted to learn. I turned my mind toward knowledge and was nearly overwhelmed with the sheer abundance that was—and had always been—at my fingertips. The flood opened my mind in a way that no other experience had before. I realized with shame that I knew absolutely nothing. I'm not even sure that I could have pointed to France on a map. But when I opened myself to learning, when I accepted that I was an ignorant fool, my mind exploded with curiosity. I *had* to learn. I *had* to know more, understand more, discover more.

I went from a punk who picked fights and drank until

dawn to someone who read two hundred books in a year. I wanted to know and understand everything about the world that I had been too blind to notice before. I began to sing and learned jazz guitar. I played in concerts and started my own band. My energy to act grew in proportion to my desire to learn. Knowledge became a kind of fuel to my ambition and work ethic. The more I learned, the more I wanted to do. Once I started, I couldn't stop. I haven't stopped learning since.

It's Not Magic, It's Learning

Imperative to living a life of performance excellence is the desire to always be learning. With this openness comes confidence, humility, and growth, because we are in a mindset that is constantly seeking new information, new ideas, and new modes of action. A learning mindset keeps us in the progress zone. To be in this mindset, we must first have the humility to accept that we don't know everything. Sounds simple, except how many times have you been asked a question by your boss or some other person of authority, not known the answer, and responded honestly by saying, "I don't know"? Often, we say anything *but* "I don't know." It's *hard* to say those words to anyone, but especially to someone we're trying to impress.

When we have confidence, we are comfortable with what we know and what we don't. We don't crumble at the first question that stumps us because we are comfortable saying "I don't know, but I want to find out."

I began working with a player I'll call Lena after she had reached No. 1 in the world juniors rankings but then had fallen into a slump of defeats that had lasted six months. I met her and her family after her loss at a major tournament. It was a tense scene, and I could see right away that the stress of Lena's defeat had affected all her family relationships. I especially noticed that Lena herself seemed almost too overwhelmed to even speak. She had lost all her confidence.

On the court, when I got a chance to watch her practice, I saw that, on a purely technical level, Lena's game was severely lacking. Her ball-striking was all wrong and her timing was off. During matches, she let her opponents dictate the tempo and flow of each point. Afterward, when we would talk, Lena put herself down. "I've got nothing," she would say, or "I'm stupid." Lena's self-esteem was absolutely shattered, a fact not helped by the way her father handled her poor results on the court. Every practice session where he was present took place in an atmosphere of stress and aggression. He would shout at Lena, who would shout back at him. Sometimes she would be so upset at him that she would hurl her racket. I understood her father's frustration, even if I knew that he was only hindering her progress. More than anyone else, parents take their child's poor performance personally. Very often they can't see that they are only making the situation worse. A player's problems reveal themselves on the court, but rarely do they originate there. To understand why Lena's performance had suffered, I first had to learn about her life off the court, because that's where I would begin my work.

When a coach puts a game plan into practice, they must do so with absolute commitment. This can happen only once all the facts have been learned—facts that go beyond a player's performance on the court. Especially when considering Lena's extremely fragile emotional state at that moment, I could have done serious and perhaps permanent harm to her game had I rushed in with a definitive plan of action—or even just "tried" a few things to see what worked. I certainly wouldn't compare coaching to medicine, but the rule that doctors must follow also applies: First, do no harm.

Many times in my career I have seen coaches force their own "style" or "way" onto a player like Lena, only to see the player get worse. At this point, either the player or the coach quits. My "style" is that I have no style. Over the years I have better defined the way in which I work with new players, but I approach every player with the same ignorance as I approached my studies in school. I must go into every new coaching assignment with a learning mindset, setting aside my preconceptions or assumptions.

The same is true for a challenge or problem in any situation: We do our best work when we first prepare by listening, observing, and gathering facts. Even then, we sometimes make the mistake of selectively choosing which bits of information we deem useful because they confirm our preconceptions and assumptions. This isn't learning; it's validating our own opinions. We aren't really opening ourselves up to new modes of thought or ideas; we're only buttressing those modes of thought and ideas that we brought with us. To truly embrace a learning mindset, we must approach the problem with a blank slate. Perhaps our previous experience and knowledge will come into play, but for the moment, we don't know that. Our job, in this first phase, is to shut up and learn. Listen, observe, and collect information. There will be time to pick through the little bits of insight we uncover, but we can't rush through the learning phase too quickly.

> Talking is a need.
> Listening is an Art.
>
> GOETHE

In many ways, Lena's lack of confidence was a benefit. When people are in such a low state of emotional health, they reveal a lot about themselves. It's in situations of great difficulty that character traits emerge with more force and clarity. Observing Lena when she was at her lowest point gave me such a rich trove of insight into her mind.

A lot of coaches would have noticed Lena's poor technical performance and concluded that was the place to start. But I knew that was a trap. Her poor technique was not structural but a function of her stress and lack of confidence. It followed, then, that to improve her game, she had to rediscover her serenity in practice as well as in competition. As I spent more time with Lena, I learned that she was afraid to fail. Her whole game strategy was to rely on the other opponent to make a mistake before she did. This is why she was playing too far from the baseline and on her back foot, afraid to attack and press an advantage. However, if I tried to fix those technical issues before I solved her fear, it would be like bailing out the *Titanic* with a bucket.

The plan that I eventually decided on for Lena included four interlocking phases. This wasn't a plan I shared with Lena; rather, this was my own framework that I would follow to focus on the reasons behind Lena's poor performance. Of the four phases, only the first one really concerns us here: Find the ideal method of communication.

To be effective, a coach needs to have a player's total confidence. This required that I learn how to communicate with Lena in the most effective way possible. Some players require constant praise, while others thrive in a "tough love" atmosphere. Notice that I put the focus on the player, not the coach. How should I communicate with Lena so that she could *hear* me?

Every day we are presented with so many opportunities to

collect information and learn from it. But the only way we can really *see* these moments is if we're engaged in active learning. I don't just listen to what my players say; I study their facial cues, their body language, their response to certain coaching methods. In the evenings, my mind ponders all these pieces of information, reviewing them one at a time. This knowledge becomes the basis of my coaching plans.

This might sound exhausting! I get it. But it's important to understand that I'm not using *learning* as a synonym for *paying attention* I'm using it very deliberately because it's exactly what I do. Little by little, I get to the point where I can hear what my players are thinking as opposed to what they are saying. It's not magic. It's just learning.

And the payoff can be extraordinary.

In Lena's case, one moment stands out. It came at a major tournament, during the quarterfinals, when she faced a top-five player. Lena, leading in one set to love and 4–3 in the second, asked me to come on the court. I walked down intending to give her some tactical advice about positioning herself inside the baseline so that she could attack her opponent on her second serves. But as I approached, I could immediately see the fear and panic in Lena's eyes. She didn't have to say anything. I could hear her thoughts. I knew (because I had learned) that telling her to play more aggressively would only feed her fear. She would view playing more aggressively as taking a risk, and at that moment, Lena would be terrified of taking a risk. She needed reassurance, because taking more risks would only increase her stress level, which was already too high. In an instant I changed my plan. I had to say something that would return her to a state of serenity, and I had thirty seconds to do this before play resumed.

"You're taking too many chances on your opponent's

serves," I said. "It's not necessary. Her serve is not hurting you at all, and there is no reason to rush. Stay behind the baseline and start each point with just putting the ball back in play, cross and deep, and nothing's going to happen."

I returned to my seat, curious to see if my plan paid off. Her opponent served and Lena stepped into the court, attacked, and cracked a return winner. From 0-15, the game went to 0-30, 0-40, and a break to love. The set was now 5-3. Lena won her service game and the match was over.

You might have noticed that I told Lena to do the opposite of what I thought she should do. I did that because what Lena needed most at that particular moment was not a tactical advice; she needed serenity. It was my mission to calm her mind, and I did this by letting her know it was OK to play behind the baseline. If I had told her to play aggressively, I would have only added to her growing panic. Instead, I let her know that everything was fine, and that is what allowed her to play to win. And the funniest part: She did the opposite of what I told her to do. She felt reassured by my words, which reduced her stress, which allowed her to feel more confident and play more aggressively. So, I told Lena the opposite of what I thought she should do, and she did the opposite of what I told her to do. In the end, she did what I wanted her to do!

> What I say is not important.
> Only what you understood matters.
>
> **DIDIER RUFFATO**

I know this all sounds like mental trickery, but the point is that it took many months of learning to reach this point where I could make a snap decision, based on nothing more than what I saw on Lena's face, and deliver the exact advice that helped her win the match. It's not magic; it's learning.

Observing Greatness

From 1998 to 2004, Bob Brett and I ran our tennis academy in Montreuil, an eastern suburb of Paris. For most of those years, it was a fruitful partnership. While Bob could devote only fifty days each year to being on the premises working with players, he was perhaps the best mentor I could have had back then. When he was there, he gave 100 percent of himself, to the players and to me. I knew he was being criticized by those inside the tennis world—the French Tennis Federation, the other coaches, the media, the corporate industry—who wondered why a coach of Brett's stature would partner with an unknown like me. But Bob never patronized me. In fact, he went out of his way to include me in his on-court lessons, teaching me his coaching techniques and filling in my knowledge gaps on tennis and, more importantly, tennis players.

While Bob worked on coaching, I oversaw scouting players and enrolling them in our academy. I also ran the entire business and recruited the tennis coaches and the fitness coaches. For the scouting part, I listened to my gut. Sometimes, watching matches at tournaments, a player would strike me as someone special. It could be their athleticism, their attitude, or a shot that I felt was very special. With time and experience, I became able to analyze the components that should be taken into consideration in terms of choosing players with the biggest potential. But even in that early time, when I had no clue, I made a lot of good choices. Some of the players who trained at our academy during these early years include Mario Ančić, Hicham Arazi, Marcos Baghdatis, Petra Cetkovská, Ivo Karlović, Paul-Henri Mathieu, Mandy Minella, Gilles Müller, Pauline Parmentier, Dudi Sela, and Sergiy Stakhovsky.

I absorbed Bob's teaching like a sponge. But if I had to

pinpoint the most important lesson Bob taught me, it would be the one that he wasn't even aware he was teaching. I studied Bob himself: how he behaved with people, especially players; how he held himself in a group of peers and controlled the conversation; and how he was able to command attention and make players listen to him. No one teaches you these things, at least not formally (though I do now with my team). Just as I spent my childhood observing my peers, picking up social lessons through observation, I did the same with Bob. He had done what I was trying to do: reach the height of the tennis world. I wanted to understand how he did it.

What I noticed most is how commanding Bob could be as a coach. He wasn't a big person; in fact, he was rather small. But he *appeared* larger than he was simply by the way he behaved and spoke to others. He had a way of commanding attention when he was speaking—an impressive feat given that he had a soft voice and always appeared calm. It was a mesmerizing combination, especially for someone like me who had struggled for so many years with extreme shyness. I had overcome my shyness by this point, but I was nowhere near Bob's equal as a confident speaker. He had a way of talking that made every word he spoke seem important.

This I said to myself, *is how a coach should act.* Calm, soft-spoken, but with an aura of authority that demands respect and attention. With Bob, you always wanted to hear more, as if he was giving you only bits of a larger reservoir of knowledge. I never asked Bob to teach me these skills—or how to be a coach. Rather, I observed him doing it and tried it out on my own.

It might seem obvious that I would so eagerly accept Bob's teaching and guidance, given that my ambitions were to have the best tennis academy in France. But choosing to learn, to listen, to absorb is rarely an obvious choice. In fact, my experience is that most people choose not to learn—or, perhaps more accurately, they believe that admitting ignorance would harm their pride and self-esteem. Perhaps they feel that asking for someone's help means accepting a subservient role in relation to the more knowledgeable person. A lot of very smart, ambitious people simply can't accept this humbling of their pride. Especially in an era where younger people have created some of the most transformative innovations and companies in the world, there exists this notion that to admit ignorance is to admit that you don't belong among highly motivated, very successful people.

There exists an alternate reality in which I might have disdained Bob's attempts at teaching me. In this world, I would have felt that Bob was patronizing me, the kid who never played professional tennis and didn't know how the tennis world worked. Plagued by insecurity, I would have deliberately closed my mind to his teaching and examples. I would have said to myself, *Who does this guy think he is? I'll show him!* And so instead of listening to Bob as a mentor and asking questions like a student, I instead would have ignored him and made player decisions on my own. Instead of gaining an understanding of how one of the best coaches in the world did his job, I would have dismissed his on-court lessons and run my academy *my way*.

Though this alternate reality was the exact opposite of what actually happened, it could have occurred if not for two things. First, I had developed my confidence. I wasn't afraid of "looking stupid" because I was hungry to learn. How would I succeed in this industry if I didn't learn from the best? As is so often the case, our attitudes, our mindsets, our willingness to listen and observe are all affected by our confidence level. The lower our confidence, the less likely we are to exhibit an optimistic attitude, an open mindset, and a desire to accept information from wherever it might come.

Second, I had learned years earlier that I knew nothing. Literally. Only when I accepted that I was an ignoramus on most topics and fields could I then open my mind and ears to the teaching and knowledge of others. "I know nothing," a concept that defines so much of my coaching approach, is modeled after the words Plato gave to Socrates in one of his dialogues, usually translated as "I know that I know nothing." The idea is that the acceptance of ignorance is the beginning of wisdom.

We enter a learning mindset when we accept our own ignorance. We listen to others; we seek out those who have come before us; we ask questions—so many questions! Never be afraid to ask questions of those who claim to know more than you. Either you'll learn that they are right and they are people worth listening to, or you will expose their own ignorance and feel better that they don't know much more than you. By listening rather than talking, you give yourself the chance to learn something. By talking, you repeat something you already know.

The "I know nothing" attitude is one of the main keys of my success as a coach, and I constantly come back to it. I have seen other coaches with this attitude whose players achieve great success, but sometimes, once they have the success, the coaches go from "I know nothing" to "I know." That leaves them knowing nothing about new players. When they use the same communication modes and methods that worked for their successful player with new players—because *they know* what works—they fail to succeed in their collaborations. They have changed their own mindset from "I don't know but I want to learn" to "now I know and will use my method."

Just as we need to consciously push ourselves into the progress zone and away from our daily routine and habits, so too must we push our brains into a learning zone to ignite our passionate curiosity. To do what? *To sustain and invigorate our need to act.* Remember, to live a life of performance excellence requires that we constantly challenge ourselves, pushing our boundaries and confidently stepping into dark, mysterious places. Only when we are in these uncomfortable situations do we grow. The same is true for our minds. Only when we delve into topics, ideas, and matters on which we were ignorant do we invigorate our brains to stay active, nimble, and engaged. A bored brain is a boring person. And unless we actively seek out learning opportunities, our brains will get bored and we will lose that passionate curiosity that makes us ask questions and search for answers.

When I listened to Bob and absorbed his teaching, I discovered that my mind exploded with activity. I was brimming with ideas sparked by gaining a little bit of Bob's knowledge. I began to understand the sport of tennis in a way I had never imagined. This served me well when Bob was away from the academy and I was in charge of managing our players. I created their daily schedules, their itineraries, their tournament appearances, and much more. I couldn't have done any of this with the level of knowledge that I had brought into my partnership with Bob. This was the key to our success: I recognized that I knew nothing and therefore needed to open my mind to learning, and Bob was happy to play the role of mentor.

Years later, after I had become a coach and had made a reputation for myself in the sport, I was doing preliminary work with Serena Williams. She had come to the academy for a few training sessions, but otherwise she hadn't officially asked me to coach her. A few days later, we were both in London (I was coaching another player at that time and preparing him for Wimbledon) when she called and asked if I would meet her for coffee. It was at that meeting that she asked me to coach her through Wimbledon as a trial. There's more to share about this moment, which would change both of our lives, but for now there is something she said that resonated strongly with me at the time.

"We don't know each other well yet," she said, "but what I have seen makes me want to take this further. I like your energy. You give out a feeling of strength. When you're in the room, even if you're not doing or saying anything, you have a presence. You also exude a feeling of confidence that makes me want to have you by my side. I absolutely want to win Wimbledon, and I'm ready to make every sacrifice in order to win. Tell me how I can do that."

I'm taller than Bob was and my voice is a bit deeper, but these are surface details. What Serena saw in me is what I learned from observing Bob Brett.

A Necessary Coach

I didn't set out to become a coach when I started my academy with Bob. It was a decision I made when Bob and I separated over disagreements about player management. I'll save the details for the next chapter, where they become relevant, and instead focus on the reasons I was asserting myself in the daily activities of the players. The simple fact was that Bob was away the majority of the time. During his absences, it was left to me to manage the players and the coaches. Because of this, I continued my education by reading as many coaching books as possible. I didn't restrict myself to tennis, either. I particularly loved the books by Tony Robbins, which tackled the idea of coaching not from a technical perspective, but from a mental and internal one. In fact, you'll find Robbins's influence on my coaching throughout this book, from the importance of setting goals to the imperative of action to living your life as a "masterpiece."

I also looked at what was happening on my courts and with my players as just another way to learn. I talked to my coaches and my players and put a lot of pressure on both in delivering results. I was fanatical about measuring the players' progress, as I saw it as the *sine qua non* of determining whether my academy was meeting its purpose. I was especially sensitive to the way our coaches taught the players, because the wounds I had received as a student had never really healed. I was determined to provide my players with a teaching environment that worked with them, not against them. Instead of trying to mold them into what they were not, I actively wanted to build upon what they already were. I was aware of the power of words and how a student might perceive them. It was clear to me that even a single sentence could live forever in somebody's mind, causing irreversible damage or inspiring impactful and positive transformation.

Most importantly, during this period of intensive learning, I kept my mind open. I didn't impose a particular style of management or coaching on my staff or players. I let the results dictate my actions. I let my learning decide the next step. In this way, my ignorance of the tennis world—its players, its coaching, its techniques, its traditions—proved my greatest asset. In any industry, but especially in athletics, the herd mentality rules. When someone finds a winning formula, everyone else tries to copy it. But I didn't know anything about any winning formula, and because I dove into the tennis world fully aware of my own deficiencies, I was ready to question *everything*.

Running a tennis academy presented me with plenty of obstacles and problems for which I was unprepared. I had business experience from working for my father, but I was in a new industry, whose rules I didn't yet know and whose gatekeepers believed me to be an arrogant upstart. With Bob at my side, I forged my way, not with any kind of plan or ultimate endpoint, but simply with a need to keep moving forward. Bob certainly brought his own technique and style to our academy, but I never looked at his coaching as the *only* way. It was one way, and a proven way, but I wouldn't tie myself to one style or one technique. I was able to turn my ignorance into an advantage because it gave me a blank slate upon which I would write a new story—a continually changing story whose only rule was to do what delivered results. I would move forward confidently, gobbling up any bits of new information and knowledge that I could use to make my academy the best in the world. Nothing was sacred except winning. Nothing was chiseled in stone except doing what works.

So, when Bob finally left for good, I was very disappointed and scared but also relieved. My relief came from the awareness that many of the players had stopped prospering under Bob's management and coaching style, and our arguments over the direction of the academy had become more frequent and more heated. At the same time, I had just lost my best marketing tool—the Bob Brett name—and a good partner and friend. Having run a successful academy for nearly six years, I was better known, but not so well known that I could use my own name—or so I thought. I decided to return to the first name I had used way back when I was renting out courts from the local club: the TETC, or the Tennis Competition Training Team in English.

Then I had lunch with one of my partners and friends, Philippe Sautet, with whom I had developed the Once Upon a Time Tennis tournament for juniors. After I unloaded my concerns on Philippe, he responded that I should use my own name for the academy. I was aghast. But Philippe was unmovable on this point: "Every academy in the world is represented by someone whose image is associated with it, who embodies the values of the organization. Look at the academies of Harry Hopman, Bollettieri, Sánchez-Casal, Evert, et cetera. You have done all the work. You *are* the TETC Academy. Now call it Mouratoglou's."

Talk about stepping into the progress zone. If I accepted Philippe's argument, then I couldn't just manage the academy. I had to *become* the academy in a way that Bob Brett had been the academy during his tenure. I had to become a coach. That was the only realistic way that an academy with my name could become a success; could be what I always dreamed it would be: the best academy in the world.

Even when Bob was still with the academy, I knew that I had been headed toward coaching. My passion had always been with the sport itself, with the players and their well-being. I wanted to give them the opportunity that I never had when I was younger. Without quite realizing it, I had opened myself up to learning all that I could about coaching, not just from Bob, but from every source I encountered. But I had been dancing around the edges of coaching because it wasn't my responsibility. It was Bob's. Now, Bob was gone, and the success of my academy depended on the success of the person whose name would be on the building. I had to become a coach. There was no other way.

I didn't have much in the way of marketable assets going into this experiment. I had not been a professional player, I was not particularly knowledgeable about the technical aspect of the sport or the physiology of athletes, and I was hardly a tactical specialist. For these reasons and many others, I had no business assuming the title of coach for anyone! And yet I had studied under one of the greatest coaches of his generation. I had eagerly listened to every bit of advice he had said—or didn't say. I also had been passionate about caring for my players, their needs, their frustrations, their dreams. I knew what it was like to be that young and to love this sport in the way they did. In the past six years, I had relied on my power observation, a skill I had been honing since I was a child, to "read" my players and know them at a very personal level. I knew that this skill, more than any other, would serve me well as a coach. But perhaps most of all, I had no preconceived ideas going into this new phase of my life. I was not stepping into coaching to prove that my technique, my structure, or my training methods were better than anyone else's. I didn't have any. I would jump into this adventure with the same learning mindset that I had had as a punk teenager who finally realized that the smartest thing he could say was: "I know nothing."

> If you want to learn to swim, jump into the water. On dry land, no frame of mind is ever going to help you.
>
> BRUCE LEE

Once I made my decision, I decided to gather all my staff to tell them the academy's new name would be Mouratoglou Academy and I would become a coach—not a random coach, but a top coach, "one of the best in the world." Sounds like bravado, but it was absolutely necessary for me. The future of the academy would depend on *my* reputation as a coach.

"But you know nothing about this job and never gave a tennis lesson in your entire life!" one of my coaches said upon hearing the news. I looked at the others. They were all clearly thinking the same thing.

"You are right. I don't know much and I have no experience in that field. But I learn very fast."

This was my answer. The very next day I was on the court as a tennis coach.

KEY 5:
Adopt a Learning Mindset

LESSON 1:
Begin with a blank slate.
When you are in a learning mindset, you must rid yourself of preconceived ideas and assumptions. This is the essence of "I know nothing." True learning is uncomfortable and difficult because you cannot rely on what you already know. Throughout the process, you will be tempted to focus on the tidbits of information that validate your prior opinions. Avoid this! Bring nothing but your own curiosity into this learning zone, and you will experience the tremendous joy of moving your own qualities and talents forward.

LESSON 2:
Seek out mentors and embrace the role of being a student.
True mentors are those who have both knowledge and experience. There is no reason to step into a new field or profession alone, except to stroke your own ego. Most people are honored to provide guidance and wisdom to those who show a true desire to learn. As a willing student, you must assume a role that gives deference and respect to the mentor. A good teacher believes in their students; give your mentor a reason to believe in you.

LESSON 3:
To learn anything, you must first understand it.
The way you understand something is by drilling down to its very essence. You do this by asking questions of those whose understanding exceeds your own. Never let your pride tell you that confusion is a sign of stupidity. And don't stop asking questions until you understand the essence of something.

LESSON 4:
A learning mindset requires action.
You don't adopt a learning mindset just because learning is itself good. You do so because you will use what you learn to act. A learning mindset pushes you into the progress zone, which is the only place where you can grow and perform at your best. You learn so that when you act, you do so with confidence in your knowledge and wisdom.

SIX

Take Responsibility for Results

It's time to talk about why Bob Brett left the academy named after him.

As we had agreed in 1998, Bob would spend only fifty days a year at the academy because he was committed to coaching his player, Nicolas Kiefer, a rising star at the time. I had accepted this arrangement as a price of his partnership, even if it wasn't ideal. Besides, thanks to Bob's coaching, Kiefer eventually rose to No. 4 in the world, which only helped attract more young talent to our academy. Despite the lopsided division of labor, Bob and I had built something successful and very special to us both.

Bob's frequent absences, however, meant that I often made management decisions without his consultation. It wasn't always practical to wait for Bob to return to the academy or try to explain whatever problem had arisen over the phone. We had forty players and a dozen coaches, and decisions needed to be made. So, I made them. As a results-oriented manager, I experimented a lot with new ideas to see what worked. One of the new ideas I implemented was to hire a "mental coach" who would be available to the players in one-on-one meetings. I was reading a lot of Tony Robbins's books at this time, and I believed, as Robbins does, that performance excellence begins with the proper mental preparation. I wanted to add this dimension to our overall coaching strategy and see if it would yield good results.

The problem was that I didn't ask Bob for his opinion. When he found out, he was livid. He saw my act as a near-unforgivable act of betrayal. From Bob's point of view, all coaching decisions fell within his sphere of operations. And rightly so; after all, it was his coaching style that we used at the academy that bore his name. At the very least, I should have run my idea by him before moving ahead with it. While I expected some grumblings from Bob, I never imagined that he would respond in the way that he did.

"No one has ever humiliated me like that," he told me. "It's as if my wife has cheated on me!"

His reaction caught me completely off guard. Had I known he would respond in that way, I absolutely would have gone to him first. But that was also why I had made the decision on my own. Bob just wasn't around. His absences made me the only person who could make decisions for the entire academy, regardless of whether those decisions infringed on his responsibilities. I said as much in reply to him, adding that I wasn't going to fire the mental coach.

Bob then gave me an ultimatum. "This is the Bob Brett Academy and I want to be in complete control of it," he said. He explained that he was no longer coaching Kiefer, which would allow him to increase his yearly attendance at the academy from 50 to 150 days—an offer I eagerly accepted. Despite our disagreements, I still greatly respected Bob as a coach and as a friend. I wanted him to be happy and to feel like we were in a mutually agreeable partnership. Especially because Kiefer had become a star, Bob's name was more valuable than ever.

Problems with our new agreement arose almost immediately. The players and coaches had grown accustomed to the way I managed the academy. With Bob now making most of the decisions and implementing a more autocratic management style, morale plummeted. Over the course of eight months, several high-level players left, including Ivo Karlović and Gilles Müller. But when my student Marcos Baghdatis, a young player whom I admired greatly, told me he wanted to leave, I knew that I had to confront Bob. "Things need to change, Bob," I said. "We can't carry on like this." That's when I gave him *my* ultimatum: change or we're finished. Bob left then and there. After six years together, our partnership had ended.

Immediately after his departure, I fell into a bit of a depression. Looking back at the sequence of events, I second-guessed every action I'd taken during the entire ordeal, wondering where and why everything had gone wrong. I even contemplated shutting things down. More than anything else, I regretted how badly things ended with Bob. He had been a good friend and mentor to me. I wouldn't have been that successful with the academy without him. To this day, my debt to Bob Brett remains immeasurable. Nevertheless, my anger over the situation made me want to blame him and his unreasonable attitude. But I came to realize that I couldn't move forward unless I understood where I had been wrong. If I was going to restart my academy, under my name, then I would have to analyze the mistakes I had made that led to this terrible professional situation—and ended a friendship.

By accepting responsibility, I was able to see the situation without my emotions obscuring my culpability. Bob had objected to my decision so vehemently, perhaps even irrationally, that there had to be an explanation for it. I eventually realized that Bob had been extremely insecure about being absent from the academy so often. It was this insecurity that likely led him to be more sensitive about changes I made without him, which made him feel as if he was losing control. He had never just wanted his name on the academy; his passion had always been to create a culture that reflected his values and coaching style. In his mind, the students were *his* players, and any coach—especially me—would have reacted badly if someone infringed on that special relationship. Seen in this light, I understood why Bob felt I was deliberately undermining him. He had felt disrespected and ignored, even though that wasn't my intention. I finally realized that I had forgotten the rules by which Bob lived his life. And in forgetting them, I learned a valuable lesson—the hard way.

But it wasn't the only lesson I learned, nor, in many ways, was it the most important.

You see, a strange thing happened when I accepted responsibility for Bob's departure. I realized that because I had been responsible, that meant I had had the power to change the outcome. It would be wrong to believe, as I wanted to believe, that I couldn't have done anything else—that our partnership was doomed to fail. It wasn't. Had I been more empathetic, had I remembered how deeply Bob felt about coaching and the academy, then I likely would have acted differently. Nothing was inevitable because I was in control of what was happening at this critical juncture in the life of our academy. Blaming Bob would have been an excuse, while taking responsibility showed me how my actions led to the worst outcome. And when I realized that I had that kind of power all along, I became even more determined than ever to start over.

Why We Accept Responsibility

Bob's departure from the academy wasn't the first time I learned how and why to accept responsibility for results. My first experience with this lesson had occurred nearly ten years earlier, when I was starting to build my academy and had gone to my father for his support. I've already written about this episode earlier, but such was its impact on me that I learned several vital lessons from it. I realized that my earlier failure as a teenager to convince my father about my passion for tennis had been my fault. Had I spoken to him in a way that addressed his primary concerns, then I would have likely convinced him. But I didn't, and I spent the next several years blaming my parents for taking tennis away from me.

My second meeting, coming as it did after I had worked for several years under my father, was conducted with my full knowledge that I was in control. The results of that meeting, good or bad, would depend on what I said or didn't say. In other words, I knew that if my father refused me a second time, it would be *my* fault, just as it had been my fault the first time. I couldn't blame him. I couldn't blame fortune or luck. I succeeded or failed based on what I did *because I had the power*.

What do I mean by that? Just this: When we realize that we have the power to affect an outcome, then we discover that we are in control of our own lives. We cease to believe that our fate depends on outside factors beyond our control, dictating what we have, where we go, and who we become. As I said at the beginning of this book, no one accidentally becomes successful. An indispensable part of living a life of performance excellence is recognizing that you are responsible. We don't wait for the stars to align just right, we don't pin our hopes on luck, and we don't look for scapegoats when things go awry. We accept responsibility, and by doing that, we acknowledge our own power.

When Bob left, I found myself alone for the first time in my tennis career. Had I chosen to blame Bob, then I would have felt overwhelmed and unprepared for the magnitude of the task that was before me. Because, you see, then I could say that *Bob* had been the key, *Bob* had been the one in charge, *Bob's* success helped the academy, and it was *Bob's* fault that the academy fell apart. Do we see how this reduces me, Bob's equal partner, to little more than a powerless observer in the eventual end of the academy? How could a powerless observer hope to rebuild the academy? How could I, who owed everything to Bob, start an academy under my own name?

This was nonsense, of course. It had never been Bob's academy; it was always *our* academy (in fact, it was technically mine, but he played a very important role on the sports side). And hadn't Bob been away for most of its existence? Hadn't I overseen the players and the coaches? Wasn't I just as responsible for the success of the academy as Bob? If I say yes to all these questions, then I also must say yes to the most important question: Wasn't I responsible for the academy's failure? And when I say yes to this question, then I am ready to learn. Indeed, to accept responsibility is part of embracing a learning mindset. When we avoid responsibility, then we learn nothing. It *feels* safer to believe that we aren't in control, but this is just us preferring to stay in our comfort zone. To accept responsibility thrusts us immediately into the progress zone, where we are open to analyzing our actions and learning from them. It's uncomfortable. It hurts our pride. But it's the only place where we grow.

We don't take responsibility for results because it's the honorable thing to do (although it often is). We don't take responsibility because we're trying to protect someone else (although we do that as well). We take responsibility because it is an admission that we alone control our fate. We take responsibility because we have adopted a learning mindset, and this is how we stay in the progress zone.

There's one more postscript to the story about the second meeting with my father. After my conversation with him, and glowing with a combination of confidence and power, I made several promises with myself, including the following:

- My future will be entirely in my own hands;
- I will seek what I need in order to get what I want;
- I will learn to convince other people and to share my vision with them;
- I will not allow choices that other people make become an obstacle to my own objectives; and
- I will learn a lesson from each one of my failures.

I was done with making excuses. From that point forward, I would make my life a masterpiece.

Find the Solution

The great coaches in sport are acutely aware of all the factors that influence results. They know they must master as many as they can to achieve victory. This isn't easy, since there are a thousand reasons why a player wins a match, just as there are a thousand reasons why they might lose. It's imperative that a coach studies every angle, because ignoring the tiniest detail might result in failure. The coach's analytical work includes the technical, the tactical, and the mental and physical condition of their players, as well as the qualities and game play of the opponent. All of it melds together to produce the player who shows up both for practice and for the championship match. Properly understood and executed, coaching is about knowing your players better than they know themselves.

The only way to achieve excellence in the coaching profession is to take responsibility for every result, whatever the outcome. Only by accepting that I alone am responsible can I engage in the extremely difficult analytical work that performance excellence demands. As such, I am constantly holding myself accountable, every day, for the results of my players. From a practice session to a championship match, I am locked in with every conceivable data point that gives me better insight into my player's progress.

Today I have cupboards in my office and home filled with notebooks of information on my players. They contain my training plans, my analyses of opponents, my feelings on different players and their progression at the time, and loads of statistics compiled during competitions. In my coaching philosophy, statistics are king. They provide me with insight that is entirely unemotional. They can deliver incisive commentary against which few counterarguments can withstand. For example, no player can claim that their backhand was "terrible" if the statistics show that they made twice as many errors with their

> The eye sees only what the mind is prepared to comprehend.
>
> **ROBERTSON DAVIES**

forehand. It's frankly incredible how we can see only what we want to see—and I'm including myself in this critique!

Given how much effort I put into winning, it's safe to assume that defeat upsets me greatly. I don't sleep the night after a loss, and usually not for a few nights after that as well. I agonize over what went wrong, and I won't find relief until I understand what happened. But I want to make something very clear: Defeat doesn't destroy me. Neither does failure. As much as I hate it, I have long since accepted failure as another moment to learn. If my player lost, then I failed somewhere along the way. In these difficult moments, I have always asked myself the same question: What could I have done differently? By adopting this state of mind—by accepting responsibility for the loss—I am ready to call everything into question and make progress. I *will* find the solution if I'm exhaustive in my review of every conceivable data point. Coaching is not about imparting knowledge; coaching is about getting a desired result. It's about finding solutions amid the horde of factors that joined together and conspired to make my player lose. And I know that when I do find the answer, I have become a better coach. I have turned the failure to my advantage and I can now throw it away from my sphere of concern. It doesn't have any power over me after that.

We can't accept failure as something to endure along the road to success. Not at all! We accept failure because we learn from it. To be destroyed by failure is to acknowledge that you don't have the confidence to learn from it and improve. The confidence I have in myself helps me remember that I will use the present failure to become a better coach in the future.

Failure is often an incredible opportunity. As a coach, I have made my best turnabouts after defeats because I always ask the same question: How can I take advantage of this defeat? Often people are more open to change after a defeat. Often people are more lucid when they are in trouble. This is the right moment to open them for a change of attitude, for a change of strategy, for a new challenge.

It is this very mindset that we must apply to ourselves, for each of us is both the coach and the player in our academy of one. As we prepare for the challenges ahead, we must be sure to cover every angle, never focusing too much on one aspect of our lives while ignoring the others. Because no one part of us is the reason we succeed or fail, we cannot neglect any part of us. Above all, we must understand that we are in control of the outcome.

To perform always in a state of excellence, it is vital to pour our attention and our efforts into achieving results. Nothing matters as much as results. We must hold ourselves accountable to the outcome, good or bad, never allowing ourselves to slip quietly into our comfort zone and claim it was someone else's fault. When failure strikes, we don't crumble. We use that failure to find the solution and press forward.

Chained to the Rules

I have made many mistakes as a coach. Some of these mistakes led to major defeats, while others led to breaking up with a player. Perhaps more so than in other professions, being a coach means you're going to lose more than you win, for the simple reason that only one player can stand on the championship podium. Nevertheless, I came into the profession with a single goal: to coach a player to a Grand Slam victory. Of all the players I have coached, only one has achieved this distinction—Serena—and she achieved it ten times as a singles player under my coaching. But for the first eight years of coaching, I never reached a Grand Slam trophy. I got close once when Marcos Baghdatis reached the final of the Australian Open, but he did not make the last step. It was my one driving passion, against which no other goals came close. As I pursued this goal with ferocious determination, I gradually and carefully honed my coaching methods, learning from each defeat and each breakup. Defeats are difficult, but breakups are harder.

My breakup with Aravane Rezai deserves a full telling here, as it was a powerful learning moment for me. Aravane was a very promising student at my academy when I traveled to Bali with her for the 2009 Commonwealth Bank Tournament of Champions. Playing in the final, she defeated Marion Bartoli (who had defeated her in the first round of the French Open a year earlier). The next day, after talking with Aravane's father, I agreed to be her coach. Over the next two months, Aravane achieved decent, if not great, results. At the Sydney International, for instance, she lost to Serena Williams in the semifinal after winning the first two sets 6–3 and 5–2, only to lose the next three sets 6–3, 5–7, and 4–6.

During this period I did my usual observing, immersing myself in Aravane's family and culture, so that I could better understand my player—her mind and inner world. What I learned was that Aravane performed at her best when she was challenged, when she saw her performance as a test of her ability and talent. Several times in those first few months together, I would deliberately goad her into proving me wrong. She always rose to the occasion, but it presented me with a challenging coaching dilemma: How many times could I use the same tactic to get the same result? I needed to devise a strategy that would both improve Aravane's game *and* continually challenge her. Whatever I devised, it couldn't be a challenge that Aravane could overcome in one match or one tournament. It had to persist throughout our collaboration, so that she felt as if she was proving me wrong *every day*. My solution would be extremely challenging, so much so that I knew there was a risk that Aravane wouldn't agree to it.

A few days before the 2010 Madrid Open, I set forth my coaching plan as a series of rules to which Aravane had to commit. They were quite severe and would push the young woman to the very edge of her limits, if not past them. I'll mention some of the big ones:

- I will make absolutely all the decisions, and if you complain, then our collaboration will stop immediately.

- I will tell you what time to go to bed each evening, what time to get up, and what to eat at every meal.

- You will follow a strict diet so that you can lose eight kilos (about eighteen pounds). If I discover you have wavered from the diet, then our collaboration will be at an end.

- Your practice and training sessions will be tougher. We will practice and train during tournaments.

- I will keep your mobile phone and allow you to use it only when I say.

- If you fail to follow a single one of these rules, our partnership will be at an end. There will be a zero-tolerance policy.

Strict, I know, perhaps even cruel, especially the "zero-tolerance policy." Aravane had tremendous talent and promise, but I had seen that she needed to be goaded into playing at her best. I knew she would view these rules as a challenge, as if I was testing whether she was fully committed to winning a Grand Slam. Would she rise to the challenge?

After I finished reading her the rules, Aravane didn't respond for several moments. I saw tears in her eyes. She knew what I was asking of her; she could already feel the pain, the suffering, the exhaustion, and the loss of her freedom. But she also knew in her heart that I was offering her the chance to perform at the peak of her ability. Never before had someone challenged her in the way that I was at that very moment.

After the flood of emotions had run through her, she responded: "I don't have any choice other than to accept. It's the opportunity of a lifetime for me."

It was then that I let her know that I would be following the rules with her. I would get up earlier than she did; I would train when she trained; I would eat what she ate. Whatever I made her do, I would do also. (And I did, losing eight kilos myself in eight weeks!)

The next day, we put the rules into practice. We were up at 7 a.m. to catch the plane to Madrid, where, upon landing, I had her practice for two hours on an empty stomach. Afterward, she was allowed to have a glass of milk as a light snack. After that, we jogged for forty-five minutes. The afternoon was devoted to intense training sessions: cardio, speed, core training. This was followed by another two-hour practice session.

When the draw for the tournament was out, I smiled. Aravane would be against Justine Henin, the four-time winner of the French Open and the world No. 1, in the first round. This was exactly the kind of opponent I wanted Aravane to play right away. On the morning of the match, I had Aravane do a session of speed work using rubber bands—a very demanding and exhausting training. But, true to her commitment, Aravane never complained once. She was following the plan.

Against Henin, Aravane dropped the first set 4–6, but I didn't panic. While she had missed a few details, she was following our pre-match plan perfectly. In the second set, she put it all together and won 7–5. My player had drawn blood against the No. 1. Before the third set began, I told Aravane to remember the plan we had put together. "Follow the plan," I said. "Only the plan. Nothing but the plan." Inching closer to victory, Aravane played her heart out, winning game after game in the third set: 1–0, 2–0, 3–0 . . . At times she turned to me nervously, almost as if she couldn't believe what was happening. I kept my face level, as if to say: "Stay focused. Don't get carried away." And then it was over. The world No. 1 didn't win a single game in the third set.

It felt like Aravane had just won a final, even though it was only the first round. I was extremely proud of her, but I had to save my praise until later, so that Aravane could continue to feel challenged. I needn't have worried. After brushing aside Andrea Petkovic and Jelena Jankovi?, Aravane defeated Venus Williams in the final, 6–2 and 7–5. She couldn't hold back the tears after converting match point. Moments later, she was standing beside Rafael Nadal, the winner of the men's title, hoisting her trophy. After that, this unknown French-Iranian player was swarmed by the media. She had pulled off an incredible upset and stood at the top of the tennis world. But when the excitement died down, it was back to work, and Aravane kept up her end of the bargain.

The next tournament was Roland-Garros, where Aravane lost a grueling match in the third round. I could see the mental and physical exhaustion setting in. The training and diet regimen was beginning to take its toll. In the Eastbourne International, she beat the top seed, Caroline Wozniacki, 6–4, 1–6, and 6–3 in the first round before losing in the second round. At Wimbledon, she lost in the second round, but then she went on to win the Swedish Open. By then she was ranked No. 15 in the world and No. 2 among French players.

Six months after we had made our agreement, following her tremendous rise over the previous year, Aravane reached the end of her journey.

"I am tired of all this," she told me one day. "What you're making me do is inhuman."

I reminded her that all the success she had achieved, rising to the top twenty in the world—an incredible feat—had happened while she was following my rules. If she took her foot off the pedal now, she would slide backward down the rankings.

"I recognize that my rules are difficult," I said. "But that's the price to pay to be No. 1. You cannot think that you will become No. 1 in the world the easy way. That is why there is only one No 1. That is why it is so valuable. And if someone can do it, it is you."

Aravane dug in. "I can no longer do what you're asking me to do."

And this is where I made a grave mistake.

"You remember what I said about zero tolerance," I said. "This will be the end of our collaboration."

She nodded.

I had been in this position before, trying to convince one of my players to keep going once they have achieved more than they expected. Some players aren't satisfied until they're No. 1, while others are satisfied with making it to the top ten, top twenty, top fifty. It's hard for me to predict where a player's true limit lies, but it exists, despite what they say when the journey starts. As a top-twenty player, Aravane was making very good money and was well known in the tennis community. She was telling me she was satisfied with her journey. Her words hurt me deeply, especially because I knew that she wouldn't stay in the top twenty for very long. There is no standing still in our sport. If you stop making the effort, you immediately drop. But she felt that she could do less and still remain one of the twenty best players in the world.

"You have just told me that you will never be No. 1 because it's too hard," I said. "That's your right. I respect that. But I want you to go to the top. If you're not interested in doing that, I will have to find someone else."

The conversation marked the end of our collaboration. Within the year, Aravane had fallen to No. 120 in the world; a year later, she was No. 250.

When I was able to look back on that moment and analyze my actions, I knew that I had failed Aravane as a coach. She had come to me in a moment of crisis. Her motivation had plummeted, and she wanted to pin the blame on her physical and mental exhaustion. Any reasonable person would have! But what was really going on was that Aravane had lost her confidence. She doubted that she could get to No. 1 even by abiding by my rules. Her doubt expressed itself as a feeling that all the effort, pain, and exhaustion were not worth it. It was easier for her to accept that than to accept that she no longer believed in herself.

I can see all this now, but I didn't then. Aravane's words had wounded me, and in my pain I clung to my rules—which had always been a mechanism to challenge Aravane, not the Ten Commandments! But I was hurt and offended. I couldn't understand why she would give up everything after all she had accomplished. Couldn't she see how close she was? Couldn't she see how much I had shared in her sacrifice? Instead of viewing the situation clearly, I let my emotions dictate my words and actions. At the time and for many days afterward, I wanted to believe that Aravane had walked away from me because she no longer wanted to follow the rules.

The truth? I walked away from her.

At that moment, Aravane needed me more than at any other time in our collaboration. Instead of being a prisoner to my rules, I should have recognized what was happening. I should have seen that her confidence was shot, and when it disappeared, so too did her motivation. I had worked with players whose confidence was in tatters. I knew what to do to get them back in love with the sport and return to the ferocity with which they played it. Aravane's crisis was nothing I had not managed before. And yet, in that moment, I lost sight of my player, focused instead on my own wounded pride, and left.

My job as a coach is help my players find solutions to the challenges they face. When I don't do that—worse, when I walk away—then I have failed as a coach. Even if my attempts to rebuild Aravane's confidence failed and she had truly hit her personal limit, at least I would have tried. Today I believe that I had the power to affect a different outcome, if only I had seen it. One of the many lessons I learned from this bitter moment, after a deep and careful analysis, is that no matter how much my player might lose confidence in themself, I can never lose my confidence in them.

Don't Dwell, Use!

In 2014, Serena Williams played in the WTA Finals, which marks the end of the tennis season. By then we had been working together for almost two years, during which time Serena had reclaimed her place as the world No. 1. The year had been mixed for us, however. Serena had won the US Open, but a back injury had hindered her in the Australian Open and she had played poorly at Wimbledon and at Roland-Garros. Many people, including me, wondered whether Serena could finish the year strong by winning the WTA Finals and retaining her No. 1 spot.

The WTA Finals uses a round-robin tourney system, similar to the World Cup, which means you aren't automatically eliminated if you lose in the first two rounds. Entering the tournament as the favorite, Serena won her first match against Ana Ivanović, 6-4 and 6-4. For her second match, Serena played against Simona Halep, my future player, and got crushed in two sets, 0-6 and 2-6.

After the match, Serena was absolutely devastated. I had seen this side of her before. More than any player I have ever coached, Serena took her defeats as personal failures. Even as I tried to deflect the blame onto me, she wouldn't follow along. She was her own worst critic. In many cases this is a good trait to have, because it means you are constantly demanding with yourself. Serena didn't believe in excuses. Like me, she analyzed every failure to find out what happened so that she could learn. But occasionally this otherwise good trait could turn into a liability. Sometimes Serena saw a defeat as a sign of a more profound failing within herself. Her world would crash down around her, and then I would have to step in and help her recenter herself.

This loss to Halep was one of those moments.

"I want to go home," she said when I saw her after the match. "I'm not ready to win. There is no point staying. I am too far from my level."

This was suddenly a dangerous moment. Serena had spent the past year and a half proving to herself (and the world) that she was still the greatest. It had been a long road we had traveled together, but she had rebuilt her confidence into what it had been when she was younger. The year hadn't gone as well as we'd hoped, but she was still No. 1. Yet the way Halep had dominated her in two sets had clearly unnerved her, and I was suddenly worried that she was about to relapse into debilitating self-doubt.

Fortunately, I knew what to say to get Serena's attention.

"First of all, you're not going home," I said. "Are you a quitter?"

I used that word, *quitter*, deliberately. More than anything else, Serena hated a quitter. To hear me call her that got her attention immediately.

"I'm not a quitter," she said, if not as defiantly as I hoped.

Good, I thought, *she's listening*.

"Second of all," I continued, "since you're staying here, you have another match tomorrow. You will win it and then qualify for the semis. Then you will play Halep again in the final and beat her."

The best way we can move beyond failure is to act. We see the defeat for what it is: a sign that something isn't working. We don't turn the defeat into something it isn't: a sign that Serena Williams is a washed-up has-been. This is critical. The longer we dwell on a failure, the more power it exerts over us and our confidence level. When we dwell, we aren't acting. We aren't analyzing. We're stuck in a moment, like a record that just keeps skipping over the same point of the song. That's when the failure begins to gnaw at us, taking little bites of our confidence. The feeling is terrible, and we allow ourselves to be swallowed by shame and humiliation. The longer we stay in this vicious cycle, the harder it becomes to pull ourselves out of it. Indeed, we will quickly reach the moment when all we want is to find our comfort zone and stay there. We've accepted that the progress zone is too difficult; that's where we fail and get hurt; that's where we make a fool of ourself and embarrass everyone who ever believed in us. We don't *belong* in that place where excellence is demanded and greatness happens. We retreat.

To pull Serena away from this abyss, I had to get her back on the court. I had to get her to see the defeat as a lesson, not a definitive statement, as quickly as possible. The only way we destroy the power that failure can have over us is to exert our power over failure. It is a lesson, nothing more. Use it as a lesson and move on. Learn from it and *act*.

Serena's next match was against Eugenie Bouchard, which she won easily, 6-1 and 6-1. It was a good victory to bring Serena back to center. However, the following match against Caroline Wozniacki was a slug fest, with Serena dropping the first set 2-6, only to come roaring back to win the second 6-3 and then close it out in the third 7-6. It was a tough match, but it brought out Serena's incredible determination. I could see the change in her. The favorite had fought her way back into the finals, where she was going to face Simona Halep . . . again.

But by then, the defeat had been forgotten. Serena had learned and moved on, rolling over Simona in two sets, 6-3 and 6-0.

Afterward, as we looked ahead to the next season, we shared a laugh over her first-round defeat. That's what we do to failure: We laugh at it from a distance.

KEY 6:
Take Responsibility for Results

LESSON 1:
Your willingness to accept responsibility for poor results is connected to your level of confidence.
When you're not feeling very confident, the reflex is always to find an excuse or put the responsibility on someone else. If you go into a defeat with low confidence, then it is likely that you will come out of it looking for excuses or scapegoats. The way to minimize this temptation is to always be building your confidence, using the techniques discussed in previous chapters.

LESSON 2:
To accept responsibility is to respect your own power.
When you shrink from responsibility, you disrespect the power you have to control the course of your life. You accept responsibility because you know that any outcome isn't ordained by fortune or chance but rather manifests based on the decisions and actions you made. You are *not* a powerless being battered about by the whims of the universe. You are powerful. You can control what happens to you.

LESSON 3:
Failure is hard, but to ignore the failure's lesson is worse.
Every time you fail or suffer a defeat, you have the opportunity to learn, to grow, to improve. This doesn't mean you invite bad results; rather, it means you are not devastated by failure. You know that the best strategy is to keep acting. You acknowledge the failure by analyzing it to see where you erred, and then you continue forward.

LESSON 4:
When it comes to bad results, keep perspective.

Bad results are inevitable, especially when you live in the progress zone. As you push yourself, the failures will mount, but so too will the successes and victories. Remember that a life lived in the comfort zone experiences few, if any, failures. And yet such a life also never experiences any victories. You exist, but you don't learn and don't improve. Such an existence might offer comfort to the weak and the frightened, but those who wish to live a life of performance excellence spurn these offerings as empty promises. Accept that you will fail because it is the only way you learn how to succeed.

SIX

Learn to Communicate

Watching one of my players "tank" in a match is one of the more difficult parts about being a coach. It's as if Humiliation and Disappointment have me up against a wall and are just pummeling my body with terrific blows. The worst part is that I have to take the beating. I can't yank my player off the court. Screaming at them won't help. Pretending it's not happening is not in my character. So I sit there, as still as a statue, glaring as my player self-destructs.

This happened with my first player, Anna, whom you met in chapter 1, during a practice match early in my coaching career. Another promising young player I was keen to recruit had arrived at the academy for a trial. She was evaluating me just as much as I was evaluating her. I decided to put her up against Anna. Anna was down 4–1 in the first set, and as happened all too often, at that point she gave up. As the points, then the games, then the sets mounted against her, her attitude worsened. It was a humiliating moment for both of us, as well as for the academy.

I left the court in a quiet rage. I needed a few moments to calm my emotions and look at the situation analytically. A lot of player-coach relationships don't survive once the player starts tanking matches. I could now see why. My frustration was making it difficult to work with Anna as a coach should. But I wasn't ready to give up. I gradually got control of my anger and started to look at the problem with a clearer head. I knew that there was a disconnect between us, a wall that blocked me from seeing the true her. I turned the situation around and tried to look at it from her point of view, then I stopped. I realized that I didn't know her point of view because she rarely communicated her feelings with me. I was getting angry and frustrated at someone whom I didn't understand.

It was this lack of communication that created situations like that practice match, where I had sent her out on the court without a clue about what was going on in her head at that moment. The solution then seemed simple enough. I needed her to talk to me. But, of course, nothing is that simple. My attempts at getting Anna to open up had mostly failed. She was a guarded person who rarely spoke unless absolutely necessary. I would consider it a good day if she spoke a few sentences to me. Some days I couldn't get her to say anything at all.

Well, that had to change.

Why wouldn't she open up to me? Why wouldn't she share her fears and other emotions with me? The answer was probably because she didn't trust me enough. We feel safe confessing to those we trust because we know we won't be judged. We recoil at confessing to those we don't trust for exactly the opposite reason: We're terrified they'll judge us.

I needed to look at this moment in which Anna had done

so poorly as one in which I could build her trust. It was an opportunity, not a calamity, as long as we both used it to strengthen our bond. As I explained in the previous chapter, a crisis isn't all bad. It often opens up avenues to course-correct.

With these thoughts running through my mind, I went back to the academy clubhouse to look for her. A few minutes later, we were in my office sitting opposite each other. I was looking at her, and she was looking at the floor. She knew.

"I played very badly today," she began. "I'm disappointed."

She was obviously feeling a great deal of shame. The last thing I to do at this moment would be to demand that she open up to me. I needed to put her at ease.

"I agree," I said. "You played a bad match. But the only person responsible for that is me. I didn't prepare you properly."

Anna just looked at me with unbelieving eyes. She clearly couldn't believe what she was hearing.

"Neither of us wants that to happen again," I continued.

"No, of course not," she said.

"Then you have to help me improve," I said, getting to the gist. "You and me, we want to same thing. If you help me, we will get there."

"How?"

"You must talk to me," I said. "You must have been especially tense before today's match. That's part of life in sports. It's not a problem. But if I don't know what you are feeling inside, then I can't help you."

She was listening, so I carried on.

"I could have reassured you. I could have prepared you better mentally. I didn't do any of that. You must tell me these things, and then we'll find the solution together."

She looked up at me. "It's unbelievable," she said. "I thought you were going to kill me!"

Why We Communicate

We humans are social beings. Communication with each other is embedded in our DNA. But it is more than simply speaking to one another; communication is how we build bonds with our fellow human beings. It's how we create friendships, nurture relationships, persuade our peers, and develop teamwork. If no one succeeds accidentally, then no one succeeds alone. I'll repeat that: *No one succeeds alone.* To live a life of performance excellence, we need friends; we need allies; we need teachers; we need students; we need loved ones. The only way I've discovered to get the people we need is through effective communication: building that link between yourself and another human being.

When confronting my player after her terrible match, I could have unleashed my anger and frustration on her in the hope that she would start doing what I said out of fear. But fear isn't how we build relationships. She had already been screamed at by her other coaches, including her father. It's why she was particularly closed off and tended to shut down in the face of strong criticism. Screaming isn't communicating. Had I screamed at her, or at the very least vented my frustration and anger, I would have built a wall between us. Coaching is about moving forward together in the same direction. We face challenges as allies, and we don't blame the other when results are poor. If I had screamed at her, venting all my rage, she would have felt even guiltier. Such an emotion would have closed her off even more to me. When faced with a crisis, we don't exacerbate the problem; we use the crisis for opportunity.

Here was the approach I followed: First, I took the blame for her bad performance. I knew it would surprise her, but that's not the only reason I did it. I truly believed it. Since we had been working together, I had failed in building a strong connection with her. That was not her fault; it was mine. I was the coach, I was the one she'd asked to make her better. If her frustration and poor attitude on the court were affecting her game, then her emotional health was also my job.

Second, I made her struggles *our* struggles. *We* lost today. As a coach, one of the best ways to generate trust from my players is by helping them carry the burden. Another way to think about this idea is that I *align our interests*. Since we want the same thing, how do we get it together, as a team? Individual athletics is a lonely profession. You don't have that team camaraderie that allows players in other sports to lean on one another. As the coach, *I* am my player's teammate. In many cases, their only teammate, in whom they must place their trust or else be swallowed by the burden of competition. We win together, we lose together, we suffer together, then we win.

Last, I showed an interest in Anna—not the tennis player, but the person. In essence, I asked her how she felt. By doing so, I created a bridge between us, a link that was based on sympathy, not judgment; on kindness, not frustration. I had to build that connection so that she didn't hide from me. Like a therapist, I cannot hold any judgment. I listen and I help her find the solution.

Critically, however, I tied my request to my job as her coach. *Help me help you.* Players want their coach to be proud of them. She was no different. But she was so used to disappointing the authority figures in her life that I believe she had long since cast aside any notion that she could make them proud.

But I was giving her another way, one that could be gained not on the court, but in the communication between player and coach, between two human beings.

How do you feel?

It's such a simple question, and yet, by her surprise, I knew it was one that no coach before me had asked her. From that point on, she put her faith and trust in me. And I had finally answered my own question: Why would a player want to be coached by someone who had never played as a professional? What do I know? The answer: I don't need to know. I will learn from my player through effective communication. Because it is not so much about knowing tennis as it is about knowing her.

After this breakthrough, Anna quickly climbed toward the top three hundred in the world rankings.

It's important to remember that communication itself isn't the goal. It's the *means*; it's how we get to our goal. And we get there by building and nurturing relationships with others. It is only through the support, friendship, love, inspiration, and advice of other people that we can live in the progress zone—pushing ourselves, learning, growing—and achieve our goals.

Effective communication with my players forms the foundation of my coaching philosophy. I have achieved greater results by building a sense of connection with my players than anything else I have tried. When I started coaching, I didn't have a lot of expertise in technique or tactics, so my only chance to become an effective coach was to let the player teach me. What I mean is that I learned what the players needed by letting them tell me—only, they often didn't realize that they were doing so. Once I really understood them, then I was in a position to help them. Off the court, my ability to communicate with others has been the source of my ongoing success in the many fields in which I work, from business to marketing to television to social media.

Indeed, discovering other people—their dreams, their fears, their motivations—is one of the most exciting parts of what I do. I refuse to lock myself into a "style" of coaching. The players determine my coaching. Some, for example, may need me to show them what to do, while others need me to tell them what to do. By creating a connection with players,

I can discover and adapt to their needs. But that can happen only when I take the time to learn who they are, where they're from, what motivates them, and what frightens them.

Tennis has proven to be an outstanding (but also brutal) training ground for developing my communication skills. Each player presents me with a different challenge, even if the question I need to answer is always the same: How do I *reach* this person? Trying to answer this question is why I spend so much time in my players' personal lives. In the case of Aravane, I shared an apartment with her family. The only way to know who people are is to understand where they're from. To take just a sample of some of the players I've coached:

- Julia Vakulenko—Ukrainian
- Anastasia "Nastia" Pavlyuchenkova—Russian
- Marcos Baghdatis—Cypriot
- Latisha Chan—Taiwanese
- Aravane Rezai—French / Iranian
- Serena Williams—American
- Simona Halep—Romanian
- Holger Rune—Danish

How could I possibly impose a single coaching style on such a diverse set of players who come from such remarkably different backgrounds? And yet that is what I've seen many coaches attempt to do. Then they wonder why their players don't listen to them! My reaction to this complaint is always the same: *Have you given them a* reason *to listen to you?*

There are only two reasons why we might listen to someone: Either we respect them or we fear them. As a coach—or as a boss or parent—it is easy enough to scare your players, but you won't get the best out of them. As any employee knows, fear will motivate someone to do just enough not to get fired. That's not good enough. We want performance excellence, and to get that level of motivation, your players—or your employees or your children—must respect you. Once respect is established, then they will listen.

For a coach or for anyone in a position of authority, respect is earned when it is given. How do we show respect? By showing an interest in a person, beyond their skills as a player or an employee. In other words, listen to them. Think about it: How many people really listen to you? How often does someone ask you how you are, but with real interest? It's incredible what we can learn from showing just a little bit of curiosity. It's incredible the worlds we can discover in another person by opening ourselves to them.

Everyone sees and feels the world differently. There is no single reality; there is just the reality that each person experiences. The key to communication is to understand someone else's world. When we build that bridge of understanding, we must do so with empathy for the other person's experiences. We must speak the language of the other person's world. Only then will we earn their respect; only then will they start to listen.

How We Communicate

People with poor communication skills struggle to connect with others. I am painfully aware of this. As a child, I watched with envy as others experienced the pleasures of effective communication: friendship, love, and joy. It was only when I broke through my silence that I could start to live life as it should be lived: in the company of others.

But to get to that breakthrough, I had to overcome my own anxieties and weaknesses to truly learn how to communicate effectively—limitations I believe many of us share. In no particular order, they include the following.

We are wary of strangers. Call it tribalism, xenophobia, ethnocentrism, it's all the same. The moment we encounter someone who is not "one of us," most humans adopt an antagonistic mentality. Clearly, this trait served a purpose when we were all parts of small bands of people, trying to defend our little bit of land from those wanting to take it. But in a modern society, one that is as interconnected and as small (thanks to air travel) as ours, we have no reason to be immediately distrustful of a stranger.

We aren't good listeners. There's a difference between active and passive listening. Most of us are very good at the latter, because that's all that's required to consume media on our TVs, tablets, and smart phones. We aren't active participants because nothing is required of us. We don't need to respond. We don't need to even remember what we've heard! We consume and move on. Active listening, on the other hand, requires effort, focus, empathy, and comprehension—all activities that engage our brains. But our active listening muscles have atrophied as technology and media have reduced our need for face-to-face encounters with real people. The result is that many of us have forgotten how to engage in a conversation with another person.

We are judgmental. When we hear someone say something that doesn't agree with our experience or values, we quickly judge the speaker. Social media, and what counts as "click bait" these days, is built on this human trait: If someone we don't know says something with which we agree, they are "good." If we don't agree, then they are "bad." When we judge someone as "bad," it is very difficult for us to ever move them to the "good" side. This dichotomy doesn't allow for nuance, it doesn't consider anyone else's experience, and it has no patience for the ethos *live and let live*. We hear, we judge, we move on.

We are ego-centric. The most interesting person we know is ourself. So many of us are lost in our own heads that we rarely give the person opposite us the attention they deserve. We think about our worries; we daydream; we wonder what they think about us. All these thoughts flit through our brains, with not an ounce of energy given to the person we are with. We can have a whole conversation with a loved one and not hear a thing they say. (You know what I'm talking about!) The person in front of us is secondary to the person inside us. And even if we hear what the other person says, we pass it through our own filter—we cannot understand their struggle.

How do we overcome these unfortunately very human traits? Well, for starters, we follow the guidelines from the earlier chapters in this book. When we feel confident, we see every stranger we meet as an opportunity to learn and push ourselves into the progress zone. When our self-esteem is high, we don't need to put others down to raise ourselves up—we can seek out contrary views and opinions because we know that we know nothing. When we break the protective shell of our own ego-centrism, we can begin to notice how little we actually know.

Becoming a better communicator is an ongoing process. Living and practicing the principles from earlier in this book helps us, but only to a point. There comes the moment when we must build our communication skills by practicing them. Fortunately, it's not nearly as hard as you might think. Here are three basic communication techniques that should show immediate results.

1. **Ask questions.** The best way to show interest and learn is to simply ask questions and show sincere curiosity. Ask open questions, which require more than yes or no as an answer. When you get an answer, ask for more explanation. Really try to understand. Ask Why?—it is one of my favorite questions: "Why did you think that way/feel that way/ come to that conclusion/make that decision?"

   Many of us love when someone asks us questions about our life, our work, our family, or our interests, while others need to be encouraged to answer. When you ask questions, you're signaling to a person that you are interested in who they are. When in doubt, ask the one question that will always get them to reflect: *How did that make you feel?* It's an intimate question, but it conveys a concern that so many of us ignore when we're trying to connect.

2. **Sympathize, don't antagonize.** Focus on the similarities you have with the person, not the differences. Find threads of common interest and build off those. Even if you need to persuade this person of your views, do so after you've built mutual understanding and respect. Use those unfortunate human traits to your advantage—help the person you are speaking with see you as a "good" person first. Then they'll be much more likely to listen to your opposing views.

3. **Observe.** Words aren't the only way we communicate. Body language, clothing, even personal hygiene all convey information about a person. This goes for you too! First impressions are part of communication, and ensuring that you make a good first impression will go a long way in developing trust with someone. Ask yourself what a person's clothes say about them. What about the way they hold themselves? What about the language they use? We don't use this assessment to judge someone; we do this to learn about them and to expand our knowledge beyond the words they speak.

These might seem like simple and perhaps even obvious techniques. But in my experience, few people bother to ask questions, too many people state their opinions too quickly, and most people don't pick up on unspoken modes of communication. As obvious as these tricks might seem, they are usually forgotten or ignored when you're face-to-face with someone new.

Beyond that, the point of communication is to create a bridge of understanding. *Get them on your side.* Then you will learn how they might help you or you might help them. Then they can become allies on your journey, fellow painters in the quest of making your life a masterpiece. Or, at the very least, they will become a new friend. Few things provide as much joy and meaning as a good friend.

Confronting Serena

"Talk to me!"

It was at this moment, during our first practice together, that I realized that Serena Williams loved confrontation.

She had arrived at the academy earlier that morning, and we quickly headed to the court. After a brief warmup, she began to hit some balls with a couple of opponents I had set up for her. She had asked to have two hitting partners and didn't want a coach on the court. So for the next thirty minutes, I stood outside the court watching her practice, just making sure she had everything she needed and people were not bothering her. As I watched, I could see why she was no longer the greatest. But I said nothing and continued to observe.

Eventually she took a break and sat down to rest and hydrate. For two minutes, she sipped water. I was still outside the court, now standing behind her, and had no intention of giving her any feedback. That's when she turned to me and, in what would be the first of many more confrontational moments, demanded that I talk to her. Serena wasn't asking; she was giving me an order.

I walked over to her, frantically organizing my thoughts. What I was about to say would perhaps be the most important words of my professional career...

That first practice was the result of a chance meeting at the 2012 French Open a few days earlier. I was there with my player, Grigor Dimitrov, whom I had known for many years. Serena and I bumped into each other outside the players' locker rooms while I was waiting for Grigor. We exchanged pleasantries and I asked who she was going up against in the first round. She said Virginie Razzano, who was a good French player but wouldn't stand a chance against Serena Williams.

Yet Razzano won. I remember the moment very clearly. I was at the Eurosport studios (where I did some on-air commentary) when the match took place. A group of us stood around the television watching in disbelief as the first great upset of the tournament unfolded. It should have been a routine victory for Serena, who was the fifth seed. But after taking the first set 6–4, Serena lost a 5–1 lead in the second, which went 5–7 to the French woman. Razzano finished it 6–3 in the third. Serena had never before been eliminated in a Grand Slam match in the first round.

Watching the match, I remember thinking that Serena was unrecognizable. This wasn't the same player I—and everyone else in the tennis world—had watched in awe as she won thirteen Grand Slam titles between 1999 and 2010. Since then, Serena had been hampered by injuries and suffered a life-threatening pulmonary embolism in 2011. But what I saw that day at the French Open told me that the former No. 1 had a long way to go to reclaim her title.

A week after the tournament, I was back in Paris spending time with my family when Serena called. I like to believe that I hid the excitement in my voice, but that's probably wishful thinking. She asked if I knew of a place where she could practice.

"I know the best place in the world to practice," I said. "It's called the Mouratoglou Academy."

Which is how Serena Williams ended up practicing on my court—and was now demanding I give her some feedback. As I've said, I knew Serena's play style quite well at that time. In 2006, I had interviewed her father, Richard, for an article in *L'Équipe* magazine, which had given me tremendous insight into the "rules" of Serena's game. And I knew at that moment that if I didn't speak to Serena with confidence and absolute honesty, I might blow the biggest opportunity of my career.

"I watched your match against Razzano," I began. "I can see you're making the same mistakes in practice that I saw you make in your match. You're not respecting your fundamentals. You're waiting for the ball to come to you instead of moving toward it. And when you hit the ball, you're not balanced. Your feet need to be farther apart and your center of gravity needs to be lower at the moment of contact with the ball to give you greater stability."

Serena digested what I had said. I waited. Then she smiled.

"My father also tells me that I don't move up to the ball. Can we work on that?"

"Yes," I said, inwardly sighing in relief, "let's go."

Wimbledon would be the first true test of our collaboration. It would also be where I would earn Serena's respect, but not because she won the tournament. Creating that bridge of understanding between the player and me takes time. It is during this time that I try to understand my player's background: the unique combination of family, culture, and environment that make up a player's world. Everyone's different. Two players can be from the same country but have very different backgrounds, especially in larger countries like the United States, where regional differences can create vastly different people. Serena, like everyone else, is a product of her background, and only by understanding her frame of reference could I hope to communicate effectively with her. And moreover, Serena is Serena. Venus is Venus. Both received the exact same education. They have a lot of things in common, but they have very different personalities. Knowing one doesn't mean you understand the other, and I needed to understand Serena.

The bad news was that I simply didn't have time before she and I were thrust into the maelstrom of a Grand Slam tournament. The good news was that Serena was also curious about me and had every intention of finding out what she needed to know. The showdown occurred after her second-round victory over Yaroslava Shvedova. The morning after the match, I met Serena on the practice court, offering her a friendly "good morning."

Serena didn't reply. She didn't even look at me. She sat down on the bench and began to put on her ankle braces. This behavior continued throughout the start of the practice session, with Serena refusing to acknowledge my presence, or anyone else's presence, on the court. Something was up, and I recognized that it was an important moment in our very brief collaboration.

Would I dare risk angering one of the greatest players in history just to show her that I'm not to be disrespected?

Damn right I would.

I would demand her respect or I would walk away.

When she sat down to hydrate, I hit her cap. She gave a start and looked at me.

"I have three rules that have to be respected," I began in my most authoritative voice. "Rule number one: When you arrive in the morning, you must say hello to me. Rule number two: When I talk to you, you must look at me and reply."

"And rule number three?"

"I've forgotten it right now, but I will keep you informed when I remember," I said.

Bob Brett once told me: "To be a good coach, you must always be prepared to lose your job. If you live in fear, you won't dare to make the right decisions and you will be weak." I certainly risked my job the moment I whacked Serena's cap, but I also would have preferred our collaboration to end than to continue on with a player who didn't respect me—even if that player is Serena Williams—because I wouldn't have been able to help her.

It might seem as if I was forcing Serena to adapt to me and my coaching style. And didn't I just say that it's my job to adapt to my players? Yes, but this wasn't only about respect or making Serena follow my rules. It was about me rising to the test Serena had given me. By accepting the challenge and confronting her, I earned Serena's respect. That was *her* method of communication. I replied in *her* language. It's not a terribly polite method of communication, but then I don't get to choose how my players prefer to communicate.

Many months later, after our collaboration had withstood Wimbledon, the Olympics, and the US Open—all of which she won—Serena reminded me of that moment and we both shared a laugh. "That was the moment I started to respect you," she said.

Those first hectic months of being on tour with Serena proved to me that we couldn't be more opposite. I had been raised in one of the wealthiest suburbs of France. Granted, my parents lived simply, without displaying their wealth, and I wasn't a spoiled child. I had my own run-ins on the street with bullies and was even mugged at knifepoint when I was eleven. But still, I cannot compare the environment I was raised in with that of the Williams family.

Compton, California, in the 1980s could be a dangerous place, and Serena grew up feeling as if there was a target on her back. I think this explains the Williams family's superhuman levels of determination. Starting with Richard, the family lived as if they were all on a mission of life or death. Tennis was the ticket out of the danger—it was the *only* ticket out. Serena carried this attitude into every match she's played. She saw it as a war: "Me or them, one of us is going home."

Now understand that Serena had this attitude *before* she became the world's No. 1. When she started, she played like she had nothing to lose and everything to prove. Being Black in a white sport, especially when playing in countries where racism was still very much alive and well, only contributed to her survivalist determination. Life or death. It was Venus and Serena against everyone. If they lost, they were going back to Compton—and there were more than a few people in the tennis world who would have been happy to see them go. Then Serena became No. 1. Did it soften her mentality? Did it lessen her resolve? Please. Her rank only made it worse—or better, depending on how you look at it.

It was important for me to understand this side of Serena, because it explains how she saw the world. This was *her* reality. And if I had any hope of returning Serena to her status as the best tennis player in the world, I had no choice but to adapt to her language and put myself in her shoes. I had to understand why she loved confrontation and the purpose it served for her. The key to remember is that Serena was fully aware that she was an impressive person. She knew she had the power to intimidate people, and those who allowed themselves to be feel intimidated would never earn her respect. And where she came from respect was everything. There was a direct line from the woman who wouldn't say "good morning" to me on the Wimbledon practice courts to the girl who couldn't show weakness on the streets of Compton.

All this eventually made sense to me, but I had to spend a lot of time with Serena to fully understand her. Wimbledon was a breakthrough for our collaboration, and I'm grateful that it happened so early. She forced an issue that otherwise would have stood between us, blocking my ability to build that bridge of understanding with her. But there was another moment at Wimbledon when Serena, recovering from a match she had just won, asked what I thought of her performance.

I knew exactly what to say.

"I haven't seen Serena yet," I said. "I want to see Serena."

Her smile told me I was speaking her language—that the bridge had been built. I think she was also telling me that we were about to embark on the journey of a lifetime.

KEY 7:
Learn to Communicate

LESSON 1:
No one succeeds on their own: You need allies to join you along your journey: friends, colleagues, mentors, and so on.
The way to acquire these allies is by aligning your interests and building a bridge of understanding with them through effective communication. Only when you have forged a connection with another person will you earn their respect and their friendship.

LESSON 2:
Open your ears, your mind, and your heart: Effective communication requires patience, compassion, and respect.
It requires listening more than you speak, asking questions, and saving your opinions and judgments. People are hardwired to spurn communication with someone new. You must overcome this unfortunate trait to communicate effectively.

LESSON 3:
Empathy and understanding creates allies: Never underestimate the joy of learning from someone new.
The person in front of you is the result of a wonderful mixture of culture, upbringing, language, and education. To discover who they are is to embark on a journey in which the rewards are friendship and respect. You might just discover that each of you are on the same journey, and suddenly a friend becomes an ally.

EIGHT

Manage Your Emotions

In 2000, when Bob Brett and I still had our academy in Montreuil, a teenage player from Cyprus came to work with us. His name was Marcos Baghdatis, and he was one of the most remarkable young players I had ever seen. I had discovered him a few months earlier at the Petits As tournament in Tarbes, France, which is the official under-fourteen world championship. I was scouting new players for our academy and found myself mesmerized by Marcos's passionate playing style. He had this remarkable ability to run around second serves without warning to hit a cannonball forehand. More importantly, he played with tremendous passion. It lit up his face and was infectious to all who watched him. I knew that with the right coaching, Marcos would one day be a superstar.

My initial assessment proved prophetic. Over the next four years, I watched Marcos develop into an exceptional player. In 2002, under the tutelage of my friend Jean-Paul Damit, Marcos reached No. 2 in the world juniors rankings. He was just seventeen. During this time, even before he and I started our own collaboration, I grew very close with him. Our academy didn't have lodgings for the players back then, so I arranged for Marcos to stay with a family I knew well. Every morning, I picked him up for the long drive to the academy. In the car, we would talk about everything: tennis, life, love, and all the worries that occupy a typical teenager.

I learned almost immediately that Marcos thought and felt deeply. This quality was the source for his infectious passion, but it was also one of his weak spots. He had the tendency to get lost in his own mind and would dwell on his mistakes and worries. I also learned that Marcos would have preferred to stay in Cyprus, rather than come to Paris. Marcos's passion was football (that is, soccer). Tennis, I learned, was his father's passion, and Marcos played mostly to please him. These were serious warning signs, and had I been able to see them, I might have been able to help Marcos avoid the pitfalls that would come to define the latter years of our collaboration. But I didn't see them—or, if I did, I didn't recognize them as serious flaws.

The reason is that I was letting my emotions dictate my decisions. In a very short span, Marcos had become my "spiritual son." I saw in him an image of my younger self, an alternate version of me in which I had been able to pursue a tennis career as a teenager. Before he turned eighteen, Marcos achieved all the things that I wished I could have achieved, and so I took his development and career very personally. He *had* to succeed.

It was this very love I had for Marcos that doomed our collaboration. Although he would reach incredible heights under my coaching, the course had been set. I was leading Marcos toward disaster. There's a reason why parents should avoid coaching their children—it's because we can't separate our emotions from our goals. Too often, we see their careers as a second chance for *us*.

When Marcos asked me to coach him in 2004, I accepted without the necessary deliberation I should have given to this major decision. He was my younger self. He was me, and this time, I wasn't about to miss my chance at greatness.

Emotion Is a Great Motivator . . .

Few would argue that emotion has no place in sports. Indeed, emotion plays an integral role in how we play and how we view sports, just as it does in many other professions. Without it, sports would be a bland endeavor and quickly bore both the players and the audience.

No one has ever created a masterpiece without emotion. Emotion, properly applied, provides fuel for the long and often arduous path we must travel to achieve our goals. The kind of emotion that most often drives us to our goals is called passion. Passion keeps us up at night and gets us out of bed in the morning. It is unlike any other emotion because it isn't reactive. Anger, sadness, joy, happiness—these feelings are all reactions to some inner or outer stimulus. But passion comes from someplace different. *Why* is tennis my passion? Sure, I can tell you the story of the younger me whacking balls against the wall in my backyard for hours on end. I can tell you about how I would watch every match of the Roland-Garros tournament with religious fervor, noting every single detail, every fault and every point to break. Tennis *consumed* me. But why?

To be perfectly honest, I don't know. There aren't any lessons that help someone find their passion. It just happens—a quirk of fate, perhaps. In my case, my parents introduced me to tennis at just the moment that my young mind was ready to receive it—like a serve. And without training, practice, or even basic knowledge of the sport, my brain returned this serve perfectly. Passion happens when our brain encounters its one thing. No one can make you passionate about something. More interested? Sure. But not passionate. It begins with a spark, and that can certainly come from an outside influence, such as a teacher, parent, or role model. But for a spark to light a fire, there must be kindling; there must be fuel. That comes from somewhere that no eye or medical device can see. I fell in love with tennis at first sight when I was four, and fifty years later, I am still in love.

This might seem like an obvious point, except that I have dropped several players over my years of coaching because they lacked this critical ingredient. The talent was there, but the fire was missing. I tried to kindle it, I tried to nurture it, but when a player lacks the passion, the competitive flame to be the best, no force in this world can give it to them. Perhaps at one point they did possess the appropriate passion, but it has burned out. That happens too. Our passions can change, sometimes frequently. In my own career, the one driving passion of my life has been tennis, but how I pursue this passion has taken many forms: coach, entrepreneur, educator, and television analyst, to name just a few.

Throughout the various roles I have held, I can see how my passion pushed me out of my comfort zone and into a progress zone. While it is life's greatest motivator, passion is also life's greatest disruptor. When you pursue your passion, you will find yourself constantly living in the progress zone. Because your passion is never sated, you continually discover new avenues and experiences to pursue. It was passion that made me reject my father's generous offer to work under him to start a tennis academy. It was passion that led me to break away from Bob Brett and eventually start coaching. It was passion that pushed me into an analyst's chair facing a camera during major tournaments. It is passion that is compelling me to open more tennis academies around the world. None of these experiences were in my comfort zone when I started to pursue them. They all tested me, sometimes to the very edge of my endurance, and forged within me a need to reach new goals.

All of it began with passion.

... but a Terrible Counselor

At the same time, emotion can lead us astray. It can override the more rational parts of our brain and lead us into decisions that are counter to our goals. A visceral, raw emotion can fill us almost instantly, like when I watched my player Anna tank a match, as described in the preceding chapter. I was beyond furious. It took everything I had not to storm onto the court and cuss her out or yank her off the court entirely. It was a dangerous moment for both of us; if I had given in to those emotions on the spot, I likely would have destroyed our collaboration.

Instead, I walked away. I knew that my volatile emotional state was driving my decision-making. My emotions were pushing me to take actions that would lead to the opposite of the goals I had for Anna and for me. Nothing good would come from me unleashing all my anger upon her. Even then, restraining emotional impulses is easier said than done. We've all lost our tempers with someone, and rarely do we not regret doing so. It never makes the situation better.

So that's the easy lesson here: We don't let our emotions govern our decision-making because we know that we will make a bad decision that will run counter to our goals. The solution—or, more properly, the habit—we must employ is to recognize when we are in a highly emotional state so that we don't make a snap judgment. Instead, we take the time we need to cool down and look at the problem rationally, with our goals guiding our decisions rather than our emotions.

Developing this habit takes patience, but there are certain things we can do to help the process. One that I've found to be quite useful over the course of my coaching career is to be the most prepared person in the room. As I've mentioned before, I spend hours poring over statistics for both my players and their opponents. Cold, hard facts tell a story that sometimes runs counter to the one our emotions tell us. Between reality and what we see of it are filters—our filters. The first filter is our conception of tennis—that is, how we see this sport—and that conception is different for everyone. We all see the sport with biased eyes. Are we sensitive to mistakes? Are we focused on winners? Are we one-handed-backhand lovers? Tennis is a simple game, but what arouses our interest in it is unique to each person.

The second filter is our emotion. For example, if we feel anxious about a player's second serve because it is not consistent, there is a good chance that his double faults will cause us some anguish. If he commits six double faults, the weight that our emotion brings to those events might cause us to feel that he made twelve. If he double-faults at key moments of the match, our anguish is heightened and we are even more likely to misperceive how many double faults he made. On the other hand, if we have a high opinion of our player's forehand, we might value his forehand winners more than his backhand winners and believe he has hit many more forehands than he actually did.

If you have ten coaches watch a match and then ask them for a debriefing, you will get ten different opinions. They all watched the same match, but each filters their perception of the match through their own biases and emotions. I have often caught myself wanting one of my conclusions about a player's performance to be true because the player had resisted my attempts to fix this part of their game. In other words, I wanted to be proved right. This is emotion, nothing more. My ego wants to be satisfied, so I ignore all other possibilities until I find the evidence I need to prove a conclusion I already came to.

This brings us to the next step in managing our emotions: Don't draw premature conclusions about anything. Not only are premature conclusions based on insufficient data, but I have learned that they are more about me and my emotional state than about the problem I'm trying to solve. Let's say I have been struggling to get a player to work on their baseline footwork, but for whatever reason the player has resisted my attempts. Come the match, I'm going to be super focused on this aspect of my player's game, and I will likely overreact whenever their footwork is off. Am I more upset that the footwork is bad or that the player resisted my coaching?

To avoid bruising our egos and keep our own biases out of our analysis, we must approach every problem from the mindset of "I don't know." Immediately after a match, if someone asks me why my player won or lost, I might have some initial thoughts, but I can't make definitive conclusions until after I've looked at all the facts. "I don't know" is how I keep an open mind. Believe me, no coach wants to get in front of the cameras and recorders and, in response to the question of why their player lost, say: "I don't know." It makes a coach look incompetent. Shouldn't I know? Shouldn't I have seen exactly what was happening on the court?

But I'd rather keep my mouth shut and look like a fool, as the saying goes, than open my mouth and remove all doubt. If I were to give a conclusive assessment of my player's performance right after a match, then my ideas would be heavily influenced by my sadness at losing, my annoyance at certain decisions the referee made, my frustration at the choices my player made, and so on. All emotion, with perhaps only a sprinkling of facts. I want it to be the reverse: all facts, with very little emotion. So I disengage, let my emotions cool, and then approach the facts with an open mind.

Preparation helps us avoid surprises. When we are surprised, our brains react with emotion—sometimes fear, sometimes joy. Let's say your player, in a tournament, draws a particular opponent that you had not prepared them for. You are surprised, and because this opponent already beat your player in the past, this surprise makes you afraid. You now have only a day or two at most to prepare yourself and your player for the match against an opponent you hadn't considered. You panic and cram too much information and hectic preparation into your player. Conversely, let's say your player draws an opponent whom you don't consider dangerous, and your surprise leads to joy. You might conclude that your player shouldn't have any problem with defeating this opponent. Instead of focusing on this match, you look ahead to the next one, believing that the current match is as good as won.

Either way, the result will be the same: In your failure to prepare for either eventuality, you are reacting to your emotions, not to the facts at hand. When it's fear, you are trying to catch up, frantically making decisions that you have had little time to consider. When it's joy, you are letting down your guard and failing to provide your player with the right mindset.

We can work to avoid surprise by preparing ourselves for as many eventualities as possible. Still, there are times when we cannot avoid emotional triggers. They happen, and it is up to us to recognize when we are too emotional to make good decisions. With my players, I am constantly studying their behaviors and words to decipher their emotional state at any given moment. This is a critical component of my coaching because it's my job to put my players in a state of mental excellence. I've learned that everyone has their own "tells" that can cue me in to their state of mind. I also ask them directly how they are feeling, and while some respond honestly, most struggle at it. I can tell by the way in which they respond whether they truly are "fine" or whether they're one bad serve away from melting down.

While it is trickier to self-analyze our own emotional state, we are not without tools. Usually, a negative emotion is the first clue—a red flag—that something within us is off. Perhaps we are tired, which is why we lost our temper so easily. Perhaps we didn't like how this person spoke to us, which is why we're dismissive of their concerns. Perhaps our player or employee performed poorly, which is why we snapped at them. Recognition of our emotional state is the first step, but it requires intense self-awareness.

It's important to note, however, that our purpose isn't to rid ourselves of emotion—were that even possible. Far from it. Moments of intense emotion provide us with incredible insight into what we *should* do, because our emotions often tell us to do the exact opposite. This is information we can use. When my player was tanking, I wanted to yell and scream and blame her for all her problems as a player. Instead, I did the exact opposite, which was to take the blame and try to build a deeper relationship with her.

Happiness and joy can be just as triggering as anger. When we're in a joyful mood, we might overlook some lingering problem that demands attention. Perhaps one of my players wins a Grand Slam. Wonderful! Both of us would be in a near-ecstatic state of happiness, which would carry over to the days and weeks following the tournament. Maybe the player gets a bit overconfident and neglects important matters because their excitement and the boost to their confidence will tell them it is not necessary to work as hard as they have been. Maybe they pull back a bit—they've surmounted one mountain, and now the prospect of climbing another just seems too daunting. And maybe I let them coast for a while. In either case, we have allowed our happiness to override our decision-making. Instead of letting our goals drive our actions, we have turned the wheel over to our emotions. And when my player inevitably crashes at the very next tournament, everyone wonders, what happened? Why did this player have such a fall-off in performance between these two tournaments? The answer is simple: By winning one, we lost the other.

Beware of Emotional Attachments

In November 2004, Marcos Baghdatis defeated Dominik Hrbaty at a tournament in Bratislava, Slovakia. Hrbaty was then ranked No. 14 in the world and was a local Slovakian favorite. Marcos was ranked No. 250. His upset victory convinced the tennis world that my young Cypriot was one of the most promising young players at that time. After the tournament, he and I decided that his goal for 2005 would be breaking into the top fifty. At the Australian Open a few weeks later, Marcos stunned again when he defeated a top-twenty player, Ivan Ljubičić, in the second round and another top-twenty player, Tommy Robredo, in the third. He was finally defeated by Roger Federer in the fourth round.

And that's when things started to trend downhill.

It started when Marcos suffered an elbow injury soon after the Australian Open that kept him off the tour until April. Then he and his girlfriend began having problems. As

I said earlier, Marcos thought and felt deeply, and his relationship troubles pushed him into a depressive mood. Adding to his difficulties was my absence. My children were very young at this time, and I couldn't join Marcos at many of his international tournaments. Marcos felt abandoned by everyone. He had never truly forgiven his father for sending him to Paris, and now he had lost his girlfriend and felt his coach wasn't committing 100 percent to him. As the months ticked by, his despair only deepened.

Marcos's attitude angered me. My affection for him was so strong that I was unable to distance myself from his actions. It was like he was insulting me. Didn't he know that I would have killed to be where he was? Didn't he know that he was wasting his gift, and that time doesn't stop? It shocked me that this young man, who came from a modest background, who at the age of nineteen was already ranked in the top fifty, was feeling sorry for himself.

How could he do this to me?

By now, readers will recognize that this is the thought of a bad coach. Without realizing it, I had made Marcos's career all about me. Instead of putting myself in his shoes and trying to understand what he was going through, I let myself sit in an angered and hurt state and decided to try to sting Marcos into action just after the US Open. I sat him down and explained that he was disrespecting his parents, who had sacrificed so much to ensure he got the best training and coaching in the world. I also said he was disrespecting me, who had invested a lot of time and money into his career.

I had turned his troubles into a rant about regret and money instead of acknowledging where he was mentally and looking for solutions. My attempt to shame him was inexcusable. But I know why I did it. I was reacting not to my goals for him (or even for me) but to my anger. My emotions had been in charge of my relationship with Marcos for so long that I couldn't see how wretched a coach I was being. Shaming someone is nothing more than revenge. Because the target of your shaming has insulted you in some way, you reach for the lowest-hanging weapon and fire back mindlessly. Is it any wonder that our relationship never recovered from this episode?

My poor attitude and coaching did elicit a productive response from Marcos, however. Angered by my apparent betrayal, he wanted to show me what he was capable of achieving. He put himself in beast mode and started to work like an animal, killing himself at practice, undergoing long sessions with intensity and fitting in heavy fitness sessions on top of it. I want to be clear that this response was both lucky as well as unsustainable. While Marcos's emotional reaction initially led to increased determination and work ethic, it was also an intense fire that would eventually burn itself out.

In 2006, in the tournament before the Australian Open, he reached the quarterfinals but once again lost against Roger Federer. After the match, as he gave me his feedback about his loss, he cried in anger. I thought that it was an incredibly good sign. Crying over losing against the (at that time) untouchable Roger showed me that Marcos's commitment and desire were in synch and at high levels. At the Australian Open, he beat Andy Roddick and, in the quarterfinals matchup, Ivan Ljubi?i?. By then, I had stepped away from coaching him and instead watched every match in the small hours of the night on my TV. He would call me after each win and ask for my thoughts on his performance. After his quarterfinals win, he asked me to join him. I immediately dashed to the airport and was there for his spectacular semifinal victory over David Nalbandian. The finals pitted Marcos against Federer, once again who won in four sets, after leading a set and a break up. Despite the loss, Marcos was the stand-out player in the tournament and the talk of every fan and analyst of the sport. His future looked incredibly bright.

And then it all fell apart. After the Open, back at the academy, Marcos told me he was unwilling to continue working at such a breakneck pace. I told him that was a mistake. I said that the explanation for his amazing results was the hard work he had been able to produce and that if he stepped back now, his results would drop. But he would not listen. He lost in the second round at Roland-Garros, then at Wimbledon in the semifinals. At the US Open, he lost in the second round to Andre Agassi, which was that superstar's final career victory. During this period, as Marcos failed to live up to the expectations he had set at the Australian Open, his father begged me to spur his son into action by kicking him out of the academy. I couldn't do that, but I also was at a loss on how else to reach him.

Matters came to a head once more in 2007 after Marcos suffered another early defeat at Indian Wells. I saw an opportunity to try to reach him one last time. Urging him to go back to work, I told him that all the success he'd had occurred when he was locked in and working hard. To which he said: "You haven't been in a Grand Slam final. I have. I know what I need to do to start again. Believe in me."

The conversation continued, but it ended in tears. Just before Wimbledon in 2007, Marcos's father called him to say that I had decided to expel him from the academy. I had done no such thing, but his father hoped the "tough love" approach might break through Marcos's malaise. It didn't. Instead, Marcos showed up at the house in England that I was renting for the tournament to tell me he was leaving the academy for good. That was that—an eight-year-relationship ended on the spot. Of course I was furious at his father, but I had to accept my own responsibility for the chain of events. I had been a bad coach.

Looking back on it after the space of a few months, I realized that it was my very closeness to Marcos that inhibited me from acting as a coach should act. Like a father that still thinks of his adult son as a child, I kept talking to him as if he was a kid rather than trying to understand what triggered his decisions and choices. I should never have allowed my affection for Marcos trump my professional responsibility. Had I behaved as a coach should behave, driven by my goals for the player, not my love, then I would have handled Marcos's depressive moments in a different way. I wouldn't have taken his withdrawal from the sport as personally as I did. I would have looked for solutions rather than shaming the player.

Today, as a coach, I accept my player's state of mind, whatever it is—happy or sad, excited or depressed. It's my responsibility to put my player in the proper frame of mind that will help them overcome whatever else might be bothering them or affecting them negatively. My job is to tackle the problem dispassionately, with clarity and distance. My experience with Marcos helped me realize that I needed to separate my love for the person from my responsibilities for the player. We act differently for those we love, just as we act differently for those under our professional oversight. Love has its place, but that place isn't in trying to help my player reach a Grand Slam. An endeavor like that requires strict focus and near adamantine resolve. We cannot get bogged down in our emotional attachments when pursuing our goals. This doesn't mean we don't love. Rather, it means that we give our best performance for those who depend on us to reach those goals. Anything less would be an abdication of responsibility. And, I would add, it is because we love someone that we strive to do our very best for them.

A State of Excellence

No player I have coached played with more emotion than Serena Williams. She is among an elite few whose state of mind alone can turn a match from a defeat into a win, as if she willed it. I didn't learn this from coaching her. I knew this long before she and I began our collaboration. It was evident to everyone who watched her play. The grunting serves; the screams of victory; the tearful breakdowns—a Serena Williams match was a cornucopia of raw emotion. Setting aside her incredible game, it was this quality that made her matches must-watch TV even for people who weren't big fans of tennis. When she and I began our collaboration, I learned quickly that my job wasn't to temper Serena's emotions. That would be like trying to soften the roar of a lion. Rather, my job was, first, to recognize her emotional state at any given time and then, second, to channel those emotions so that they powered her toward her goals.

There was a downside to this raw emotional energy, of course, which I saw after her first-round defeat at Roland-Garros shortly before we started working together. Serena couldn't handle defeat, at least in her state of mind at that time. All champions must overcome the devastation of defeat, and at one time Serena had that ability to bounce back. But not in this case. She had lost the ability to use defeat to launch herself toward victory. Instead, she saw defeat as a sign that she could not win a major tournament anymore, and that she was running out of solutions. She decided that something needed to change in order to start winning again.

That change occurred at Wimbledon a month later. Serena won the tournament, which cemented our official collaboration. But I'd be a horrible coach if I saw Wimbledon as marking the end of Serena's troubles. Again, we can't let momentary victories cloud our judgment. I knew that Serena had a long way to go before her mental state could match what it had been during her dominant years. Winning a Grand Slam might have been good enough for other players; it might have been good enough for the Serena Williams I had started to coach. But for the Serena Williams of her dominant years, the woman who had taken the sport of tennis by storm? No, not anywhere *near* good enough.

It was an attitude that Serena herself had to remember and embrace once more. During that Wimbledon tournament, she joined me in the players' restaurant after winning her fourth-round match, absolutely beaming.

"Patrick," she began breathlessly, "whatever happens, I will be in the top three in the world at the end of the tournament."

She had just given me an opportunity to start the process of banishing the Serena I had met after Roland-Garros.

"So what?" I replied. Her face fell.

"Aren't you happy about that?" she asked.

"No," I said simply. "I couldn't care less."

That got the reaction I wanted. "Excuse me?"

"Serena," I began, "for someone like you, being top three in the world is just a stage you must pass through. It's a symbol of your recent troubles and decline. It's not the final goal. I won't be happy until you're No. 1." The underlying message here was: *You* shouldn't be happy until you're No. 1 again.

Serena chewed over my words for a moment before leaving. (Incidentally, this is exactly how we should react when someone triggers our temper: *Wait. Think.* Then respond.) She walked away in obvious shock. I knew I had hurt her in her most vulnerable spot. I had meant to. By reminding her of who *she had been*, I was setting the bar at a height that Serena had to—but didn't yet—believe she could attain. It was nothing more than telling her that my job as her coach wasn't to "get close" to the old Serena. It wasn't even to get equal with the old Serena. It was to surpass the old Serena. My goal was helping Serena become the greatest player of all time. But it would happen only if that was *her* goal as well. The old Serena would throw a second-place trophy in the trash after a match because it was just a reminder of her failure. I needed *that* Serena to come back, the one for whom being No. 1 in the world was the only goal worth achieving.

Later in the day, she texted me her response. "You're right about the rankings," she wrote. "I don't even understand how I could be happy about it. No. 3 is worthless. Even No. 2 is worthless. No. 1 or nothing!"

Welcome back, Serena.

Rebuilding Serena's state of mind required a conscious effort on my part. I had to put in place a long-term program whose focus was on re-creating the state of excellence Serena had operated under in the first part of her career. As you might expect, this wasn't simply a matter of improving her technique or tactics, although that was certainly part of it. Rebuilding her confidence in her own dominating play style was always a central part of the plan. But a more important part—the part that all other elements of the plan would build upon—was reprogramming her mind so that her raw emotional energy worked for her, not against her.

The first piece of the puzzle was to reestablish Serena's confidence. I have never met anyone who was as confident in themselves as Serena Williams. But when we started working together, her confidence was shot. Not even some Wimbledon victories could fix it. I could see the continuing frustration, borne from a lack of confidence, that would grip her during a bad match. One of Serena's greatest assets was also one of her greatest liabilities. She simply could not accept defeat. On the court that frustration became tension and stress, both of which can be very damaging. I had to help her change this part of her.

I knew that Serena had great faith in me. With that in mind, I knew that my own attitude and everything I said—positive or negative—would affect her confidence. If, for instance, she asked me during practice what she needed to work on, she was really asking whether I believed in her. She wanted to be sure that I saw the champion inside her. I could still offer criticism and advice, but it had to be done in a way that told her I had no doubt about her game. "Tough love" doesn't work on Serena as it might on other players. If I employed it on Serena, it would have crushed her spirit. Instead, I boosted her with affirmation constantly. And because she valued my judgment, she could believe in what I said.

Second, I had to reduce Serena's stress levels, which threatened to swallow her whole. The prospect of having to reclimb a mountain that you already know is nearly impossible would stress out anyone, and Serena was no exception. Much as I had done with other players, I had to establish in her mind a "midterm perspective." Namely, I wanted her to forget winning Grand Slams over the next few months and focus solely on rebuilding her game and confidence. What I was really saying was that it was OK to lose ... for the moment. Remember, Serena never handled defeat well, so this wasn't an easy task. But the rebuilding phase would take time, and I needed her to be patient. Accepting, on a temporary basis, the idea of defeat freed her from her anguish. She didn't have to worry about the impossible mountain, just the next step in front of her. By removing the pressure to perform in each tournament, I could reduce the overall pressure that was debilitating for her.

But, again, the absolute best way to minimize and manage stress is through preparation. You must understand that a professional tennis player lives in a world of unknowns and strange environments: She travels all over the world, spending a significant chunk of her life on a plane or in a hotel room; she doesn't know who her opponent will be from one day to the next; she is unsure of the weather conditions; and on and on. In short, all the things that would stress out any normal person are magnified in the life of a tennis player. The *best* way to minimize this anxiety is for the player to strive for perfect preparation. What is perfect preparation? I define it as identifying and studying all the factors that we can control in our sphere of life or work. We remove the unknowns from the tally. We focus only on what we can control. As a coach, my job is to strive for perfect *mental* preparation for my player. Obviously, nothing is perfect, but I want my player to believe that when I brief them on their opponent, I am providing them with the best possible information and analysis. When they step foot on the court—in a strange country, on a crappy weather day, against an opponent they've never faced—they at least believe that they are as prepared as they can be to win the match.

Every time Serena stepped out on the court, she knew where her opponent generally placed their serves in each service box, on both the first and second serve; what her opponents' strengths and weaknesses were; their usual playing patterns and those patterns in which they were most uncomfortable; how they played during important points; their playing behavior when they were ahead or behind; and so on.

When I briefed Serena on the day of a match, I would know her state of mind precisely. I knew the exact words I would use to play off those emotions roiling inside her and put her in a state of performance excellence.

The goal I had for her is the same goal I have for you. We don't run from our emotions. We recognize them. We learn from them. We deal with them in whatever way we must.

Sometimes that means we step away; other times that means we push ahead. But we never let them overpower our decision-making. We never let them obscure our goals. And when we've learned to master them, that's when we have entered into a state of performance excellence.

The summer after Wimbledon was a busy one for Serena. After her win there, we stayed in London for the Olympics, taking home gold in both the singles and doubles categories. From there, we went to New York and won the US Open, then finished the year winning the WTA Championships. For any other player, that would have been a career-defining year. For Serena Williams? It was a good start.

KEY 8:
Manage Your Emotions

LESSON 1:
Emotions are the juice of life.
They make you laugh, they make you cry, they make you sing, and they make you create masterpieces. But unbridled emotion can also lead you down the wrong path, away from your goals. As you move forward, you must learn how to recognize your emotional state at any given time and the reasons why you feel the way you do. You must build your self-awareness to the point that you can recognize when you're about to make a decision influenced by your emotions rather than the facts.

LESSON 2:
To master your emotions, you must reduce the triggers that can lead to emotional outbursts.
Far and away the best method to accomplish this is to prepare for as many eventualities as you can. Surprises are moments when your emotions tend to go haywire. Thus, as part of your mastery over your emotions, you can reduce those surprises through preparation.

LESSON 3:
Emotional attachments can often lead you astray.
You likely treat those you love differently from those with whom you work, so it is generally unwise to mix the two. Love clouds your judgment, and you often cannot separate your concern for someone close to you from the pursuit of your goals. To achieve your goals, you often must be brutally honest, singularly focused, and resistant to distractions.

LESSON 4:

Your purpose isn't to rid yourself of emotions; rather, it is to manage your emotions and learn how to make them work for you.

When you strive to always perform in a state of excellence, then you must learn how to focus your mind without destroying your passion. Because emotions can be your best friends or your worst advisors, recognize the ones that bring you enthusiasm, confidence, and a willingness to work—the ones that put you in motion. Whatever activities or thoughts trigger those emotions, use them!

NINE

Your Entourage Matters

In the fall of 2022, Simona Halep was finishing a tumultuous season on the court. After starting the year with a victory in the Melbourne Summer Set, she had stumbled through much of the first half of the year before asking me to coach her. I accepted, and together we reached the semifinals at Wimbledon (which she had won in 2019). In August, Simona finished strong in the WTA 1000 tournament by winning her twenty-fourth title, which catapulted her back into the top ten at No. 6. After losing at the US Open in the first round, Simona, struggling with injuries and other medical conditions, announced she would sit out the rest of the year.

As her coach, I was happy with her progress but knew she had a lot further to go. Since being ranked No. 1 in 2017, Simona had had a career defined by incredible highs and some pretty devastating lows. She had won two Grand Slams—Wimbledon and the French Open (in 2018)—and had lost in the finals at the Australian Open, also in 2018. A calf injury in 2021 sidelined her for the French Open and Wimbledon, after which she dropped out of the top ten for the first time since 2014. The following year—the year we started our collaboration—Simona reclaimed some of her former dominance until once more being knocked down by injuries.

Then, in October, the letter arrived. Simona called me immediately.

"I've tested positive for a substance I never heard about: roxadustat," she said, panic in her voice. She didn't need to explain further. The International Tennis Integrity Agency (ITIA), the governing body that works with the major tennis leagues as well as the Grand Slam tournaments, has banned roxadustat as a performance-enhancing substance. Neither of us knew how it got into her system. What we did know was that Simona was innocent. Not that it mattered. Until her hearing, Simona was officially suspended from all major tennis tournaments. Just like that, my player's tennis career was all but over.

Hyperbolic? Hardly.

To understand why, you must first realize that the damage a positive test does to a player's career cannot be overstated. It's very much a "guilty until proven innocent" system, where perception counts far more than facts. As the news spread rapidly through the tennis world, Simona was increasingly isolated from the community she loved. The shame itself was all-consuming. Simona felt it from the media and from her sponsors, all of whom eventually fled. As the months dragged on, she lost her motivation to practice. She believed she would never play again. In my darker moments, I found myself losing hope too.

All Simona had left were her closest friends, her family, and her coach. As it would turn out, that was all she needed.

The Support We Need

Some years ago, I was speaking with a fellow coach whose player had reached the top ten in the rankings after many years in the top hundred. That was a big move! I congratulated him on the great work he had done. He laughed.

"It's not me," he said, "it's his girlfriend."

"Seriously?" I asked.

"Yes. He is so in love with her. She is so in love with him. She looks at him like a god," he said. "She gave him so much confidence in himself! It is incredible."

I dwelled on this lesson for a long time, trying to decide if there was anything to it. Surely there was a better explanation for this player's spectacular rise than a doting girlfriend! How big an impact could this component have on a player's performance? I kept the question in the back of my mind, but it wasn't until some time later, when one of my own players had an opposite experience, that I put things together.

In my player's case, the relationship he had with his girlfriend was a point of continual frustration for him. I could tell that he didn't reciprocate her love. Normally these things are none of my business, but I began to see his performance on the court suffer. I tried various strategies to pull him out of this funk, but eventually I realized he was bringing that relationship frustration with him to the court. I sat him down one day and asked him why he was still with this woman, given that it was obvious he didn't love her. He didn't have a good answer.

"She's frustrated all day long, because you don't return her love," I said. "Because she is suffering, all she gives back to you is her frustration, instead of lifting you up, giving you love and admiration. How can you feel good about yourself? Also, deep inside, you know you should end it because the point of a relationship is to inspire each other and feel stronger together than if you were alone. In this case, she brings you down you because you cannot give her what she needs: your love. Something must change."

He agreed with me and said he would end things with his girlfriend. When he did—when he removed that source of turmoil and negative energy from his life—he began to play better. Much better. By this point, I was convinced that what my friend told me earlier was true: There is direct correlation between the people in our lives and our performance. The idea that we can separate work from life is nonsense. Those who try to keep them separated, those who believe that they can shield their work life from their personal life, are deluded. And since this is the case, then it stands to reason that we should strive to surround ourselves with people who support us, *who make us better.*

Have you ever wondered why celebrities and great athletes always seem to be surrounded by a group of friends, known—negatively, I should add—as their "entourage"? We tend to dismiss these people in the star's orbit as sycophants or bootlickers. But I have seen many examples of star players who surround themselves with people who are not flatterers or groupies; they are the player's strongest supporters and biggest believers. They don't tell the players what they want to hear, they support them. They are friends who can pick them up when they are down.

A lot of our misconceptions about a star's "entourage" stem from the idea that they can't handle criticism. This is absurd. In my experience, no one was ever more critical of Serena than she was herself. The same holds true for every other great athlete or high-achieving person I have met. They are constantly evaluating their own performance. It is an obsession. Their inner monologue runs day and night, filling them with all manner of negative emotions and, in some cases, despair.

Stars aren't immune to imposter syndrome, the feeling that they don't deserve the success they have achieved. It gnaws at many of them. The effect of this highly attuned self-awareness is doubt. Serious doubt. To counteract this level of strain and self-criticism, high-achieving individuals rely on those around them to remind them of their ability and worth. I know how that sounds; it's egotistical; it's pampering; it's pathetic. And yet very few people have experienced life at the very pinnacle of their profession. Successful people don't surround themselves with their most fervent supporters because they're addicted to praise; they do it because they are consumed with doubt.

Here's the trick, though: You don't need to be the greatest tennis player of all time to emulate that player's tactics of living in a state of performance excellence. Anyone can—and should—do it.

Our Inner Monologue

I recall a match I played at the academy not so long ago. On the sidelines was a friend of mine whom I have known since we were schoolmates. As the match progressed, I began to lose. My friend, seeing my frustration, tried to sound encouraging by giving me excuses for my impending defeat: "He's so much younger than you, Patrick. You should be proud that you're even keeping the match competitive." And so on and so on. I felt those excuses creeping into my own focus, derailing my determination to win at any cost. Maybe he was right . . . maybe I had no chance against this younger player.

My brain greedily gobbled up my friend's excuses and felt perfectly legitimate. I slipped so easily into a defeatist mentality. While trying to be helpful, my friend was sabotaging me. That's why I snapped.

"Shut up! I don't want to hear excuses. I am going to win that match!" I finally told him during a break in the match. My confidence was fighting to return. I didn't need excuses for a defeat. I needed to know that I could win. My friend, cowed by my ferocity, did in fact shut up, and I got down to the business of winning the match. Like I knew I could.

Here's another example: On my social media feeds, I often post educational videos that discuss tennis technique and strategies. Since I was a boy, my forehand has been my best shot, even though my technique isn't exactly "proper." I don't care; it's worked for me and so I never bothered to fix it. Also, ten years ago, I tore a ligament in my wrist, and as a consequence, my wrist is not as stable as it should be. To avoid hurting it, I decided to hold my grip tighter so that my wrist would be more blocked and thus less loose. The new grip prevents my wrist from doing the the "whip effect," in which a powerful wrist thrust really smake a shot. But because of the injury, I have no other options.

However, when I would post teaching videos, the comments section would be inundated with criticisms of my forehand and all the ways in which my technique was awful. I know the golden rule about social media is to avoid reading the comments, but I enjoy seeing how viewers respond to our videos. At first I just ignored the criticisms of my forehand—or at least I thought I did. Then I noticed, on the court, how I started to question my forehand. I started to think about it in a way that I never had before, and just like that my forehand lost its power. My best weapon was rendered harmless because I couldn't stop thinking about my technique. The negativity from mere strangers had such an impact on my inner monologue that it ruined what had been a perfectly good forehand shot.

Now imagine this kind of negativity from someone close to you: a friend, a loved one, a boss, or a coach. When those closest to us criticize us in ways that weaken our resolve or make us question our decisions, we lose our confidence. We start to think about things that we never had to think about before. And, usually, when we start to (over)think about things that are challenging, ambitious, or outside our comfort zone, we lose our resolve to try them.

What do we tell a kid who is afraid to jump off the high dive at the pool?

"Don't think about it!" we shout. "Just jump!"

But we all know that the longer a kid looks over the edge of the diving board, the less likely they are to jump. The kid is thinking about it, and that rational part of the brain is busily finding all the reasons why jumping is a bad idea. The kid might still do it, listening to the encouragement of friends and parents. But the line between action and inaction is thin. All it would take to make that child back away from the edge and climb down the ladder in defeat is *one* person to tell them they shouldn't.

It's strange the way the mind works like that. When faced with a challenge or dilemma, it is most impressionable to outside forces—like negative comments from friends or even strangers—and it reacts to these forces by creating doubt. Perhaps this is some vestige of our innate survival instinct at play. Humans are social beings, and if our fellow humans are telling us not to do something, we are generally inclined to believe it. So our desire or motivation to try something new and challenging, to step outside our comfort zone, withers, affecting our inner monologue, until we say, "Eh, that probably wasn't for me anyway." It doesn't even take that much—one person saying "you can't" can override a hundred people saying "you can." How many dreams have been crushed by the "practical" advice of our friends, colleagues, and, yes, strangers on the internet?

To move forward, to get out of our comfort zone, we must do two things. First, we need to train our inner monologue to see risk as a reward, not as a threat. Second, we need to surround ourselves with people whose voices work *with* our inner monologue, pushing us forward, picking us up, constantly challenging us to tackle new heights, not against it. Especially because our inner monologue will surely fail us—we will begin to doubt our ability—those outside voices from people we love will be the only deterrent from a life lived in the comfort zone. Easier said than done, but there is a way.

Retraining Our Mind

When a dog develops anxiety in a certain situation, like a thunderstorm, the most common mistake an owner makes is to coddle the dog. With our touch and our words, we try to soothe the dog to calm its anxiety. This might relax the dog during the thunderstorm, but it won't solve the problem. When the very next thunderstorm rolls through, the dog will be as anxious as before. Why? Because our soothing methods only reinforce in the dog's mind the idea that thunderstorms *are* dangerous and the dog *needs* coddling. The dog will never overcome its fear of the sound and fury of a thunderstorm if it knows that its loving owner is going to rush in to give the dog comfort and love.

The solution? During a thunderstorm, the owner should act like nothing is wrong. We don't run to the whining, whimpering dog. We don't do anything. Over time, our normal behavior will convince the dog that there isn't anything to worry about.

Such in dog training, so in tennis. When players are in doubt, bad coaches will try to reassure them before matches.

"Yes, you're playing well," the coach says. "Don't worry!" The coach wants to soothe the player, even though this doesn't do anything for the player's confidence. It reinforces the idea in their head—that constantly running inner monologue—that they need comforting because their opponent is out of their league. A coach's task isn't to quiet the anxiety and doubt; it's to raise the confidence of the player, to change that inner monologue from doubt to belief. We don't say, "This is a really big match, so you can't make any mistakes!" Worthless advice. If a coach has done their job well, then the player should know what they need to do to beat this particular opponent—not because this opponent is out of their league, or No. 1, or because this is the finals of Wimbledon, but because this is what we practiced and it's the player's job to execute the game plan. "Do these things right, just as we practiced, and you will win" is the best distillation of my pre-match talk. Speak to a player's confidence, not to their worries.

I had to learn this lesson with my players the hard way. Early in my time coaching Marcos Baghdatis, we entered a tournament in Bratislava, Slovakia. Marcos was then ranked three hundredth in the world, and so when he reached the finals against the No. 14 player, Dominik Hrbaty, I was overjoyed. Then the match started . . . and started badly for Marcos. It was still the first set and Marcos was down 4–1. At that very moment, I was assailed by negative thoughts: "Marcos can't win. He's completely outmatched." I had lost confidence in my player. My inner monologue was a running stream of negativity: "Hrbaty is so much stronger than Marcos. He serves better, has a better forehand and a better backhand, moves better, and makes fewer mistakes." The negativity quickly turned to resignation and excuses: "A defeat isn't so bad. It's a victory even making it to the finals. Marcos should be pleased." And on and on.

What a wretched way for a coach to think. Fortunately, I kept these thoughts to myself and tried to coach Marcos despite my own inner monologue. And then Marcos won the match and the title. In a stunning upset, Marcos fought his way back into winning both sets, 7–6 and 7–6. I was suitably humbled. After the final, I promised myself that I would never again entertain these kinds of limiting, defeatist thoughts. I would *will* myself into being my players' biggest supporter, believing that they are capable of accomplishing anything and beating anyone. I would not allow myself the luxury—the comfort—of excuses. By accepting them as my players, I was telling them: "I believe in you 100 percent."

More importantly, I began to enforce these tactics among the people in a player's life: their friends, family, and love interest. I don't condone *any* negative talk around one of my players. I often have to step in and tell a player's circle of friends that if they say one negative thing to the player, they are out. It sounds harsh, but they get the point. This rule applies to parents as much as it does to friends. My motto for this kind of coaching is simple: "By fixing my gaze on your weaknesses, I weaken you. By focusing on your qualities, I strengthen you."

We must adopt this same mantra for ourselves. It is so easy to drift into negativity because that's what our inner monologue is preprogrammed to do. It is a defense mechanism, designed to keep us from taking foolish risks. But the same mechanism also keeps us from taking on greater challenges. Trying to squash this innate part of our thinking will take time. It will feel uncomfortable. We will believe we are frauds. But we must continue to practice it until we've reprogrammed our inner monologue to focus on our qualities, not our weaknesses.

One of the ways in which I reprogrammed my own inner

monologue was to notice when I was thinking negatively. I would pull out a notebook and jot down my negative thoughts as they occurred. Over time, as I continued this practice, I could detect patterns in my inner monologue, triggers that would start a negative cycle. Much of this book is about pulling ourselves out of a negative cycle and entering a virtuous cycle. I couldn't have done it myself had I not been made aware of my own inner monologue's own patterns.

What are you saying to yourself? What is the conversation you keep having with yourself? I will bet you it's something negative. Until you've reprogrammed your inner monologue, all it does, all day long, is spit negative thoughts at you. If you keep saying these things to yourself, you get the same result. The only way to get a better outcome is to change the language. So, bringing us back to tennis, if you miss a break point and you tell yourself "I can't convert a break point," then you won't. Instead, replace that thought: "I can't convert all the break points anyway. So I'm going to create another break point, and another one, until I do it."

The next thing we must do is replace the negative thoughts you have written down with positive ones. There's an easy formula for doing this too. I can almost guarantee that most of the negative thoughts you have during the day have "can't" in them: "I can't do this," "I can't do that," "I can't catch a break," "I can't lose weight," "I can't get a date,"... You get the idea. The solution—the positive replacement—is obvious: Replace "can't" with "can." That's it. So, "I can't lose weight because I don't have time to exercise" becomes "I will lose weight by walking to lunch every day." That's the secret to how we start reprogramming our inner monologue. It's not the end point, however. In time, if you stick with this simple plan, you will be able to find the positive opposite of some of your most pernicious negative thoughts, those insecurities and fears you have held on to since you were a child. In this way, you can transform your inner monologue into a force that pushes you into the progress zone.

Remember, our inner monologue is designed to keep us safe. It abhors risk and challenges. It seeks solace and comfort. It is the dog whining in fear of the thunderstorm. Our instinct is to save the dog. Help it. Soothe it. Comfort it. We do the same with ourselves. When we tell ourselves we can't do something, we are wrapping ourselves in the soothing embrace of the comfort zone. It's warm, it's cozy, it's safe—and it's where you will never grow.

A Challenge Unlike Any Other

In twenty years of coaching, I had never had to deal with one of my players testing positive for a banned substance like roxadustat. But in those twenty years, I had developed a coaching method that was simple and straightforward: I am there for my players 100 percent. That is the essence of coaching. All the philosophies, slogans, and mottoes—they all boil down to this very clear method. I will never let my players down. More than that, I will never give my players a reason to doubt themselves. It is *my* job to be their most fervent supporter.

It was with this attitude that I entered a nightmare beside Simona. Neither of us knew what to expect, so I reached out to players who had gone through a similar ordeal. Their message was both clear and terrifying: "Be prepared for the worst." They were right. As the days and weeks and eventually months dragged on, Simona's resolve to clear her name nearly broke. I eventually learned that the delay was all by design. The organization that tests players and hands down punishments has every incentive to prolong the process for as long as possible. They want a player who has tested positive to give up the fight, because it saves them the trouble of proving their allegations and helps to prove their effectiveness as an organization.

Our first task was to figure out how to clear Simona's name and disprove the test results. We learned that if we were unable to document how micrograms of roxadustat ended up in her system, she would be banned for four years. In other words, the ITIA did not have to prove her guilt, but we had to prove her innocence. That sent us scrambling for doctors and scientists who could guide us. The consensus among the scientific and medical team we brought together was that the positive result was likely caused by contamination. Meaning, the banned substance was present in another product (an authorized one) Simona had used. The working theory then became that the product was contaminated at the factory. The amount of roxadustat found in Simona's system was so small as to be almost imperceptible—*almost*. The ITIA doesn't consider quantities when ruling on positive results, only the presence of a banned substance.

We then tested every supplement, vitamin, and personal care product that Simona used on a regular basis to find the source of the contamination. Further investigation showed that the collagen product a member of my team had recommended to Simona was the likely culprit. There was no way I or my team could have known that this product had been contaminated with roxadustat, but the discovery came after months of investigation. (This issue is becoming more frequent. In 2024, a top player took a medicine that had been contaminated and then tested positive for a banned substance.) We sent word of our findings to the ITIA. They reported back that their testing of the collagen product turned up no trace of roxadustat. In September 2023, ITIA announced its findings that Simona had "intentionally" used a banned substance and handed down a four-year suspension. For a player in her early thirties, the news sounded the death knell for her career.

It had been a year since the original test had come back positive and we were all exhausted by the fight. I told Simona I would be more than willing to stand before the cameras and tell the world that I was at fault. Sometimes standing by your player no matter what means you take the fall. That's the reality. So in November 2023, I released a video on Instagram in which I took responsibility for the hell that had consumed Simona's life and threatened to end her career.

We were not finished, though. We knew the truth was on our side; it was just that the journey was proving more difficult than we could have possibly imagined. It is during moments like these that our inner monologue can potentially become our worst enemy. No matter what we might have done to reprogram it, very few people can suffer through what Simona suffered and remain optimistic. Every rational thought told her—and us—that continuing the fight was useless. We were outmatched in nearly every way. The ITIA acted as both prosecutor and judge, a blatantly unfair arrangement that meant their experts were always right and ours were always wrong. The search for the truth was replaced by the search to prove the guilt of someone who was a victim of a contamination—and this with nearly unlimited resources, access to labs and tech we could only dream of, and control over the very hearings that could clear her name. On Simona's side, we had assembled a great team, but how much longer could we fight what then seemed to be a losing battle?

And this is where your entourage can save you. The people closest to Simona—her family, her friends—did not let her forget who she was: a Grand Slam champion and one of the best players in the world. This wasn't past tense. This was her present, and it would be her future. There was no way they would let her career end on the whims of a organization that seemed hell-bent on destroying her. They would stand by her and fight until every last opportunity and avenue of hope had been exhausted. From my perspective, what was most impressive about Simona during this time was her attitude. No wonder she was a champion; she showed it in every possible way. If this was her last tennis match, at least she would play it to win. She would go down swinging her racket. During competition, there are ups and downs, and there are moments in which you can lose faith. But the remarkable thing with Simona was that those moments of losing faith very soon gave way to determination. She refused to lose.

Our final chance came in February 2024, during a three-day hearing before the Court of Arbitration for Sport (CAS). We once more presented all our evidence to prove that Simona's positive results came from contamination. And that was it. Our last hope. On March 5, the CAS released its findings, which agreed that contamination was the likely culprit. It further stated that a multiyear suspension was inappropriate and cleared Simona to play immediately.

We had won—and now it was back to work.

Surround Yourself with Support

It is often said that no one goes through life alone. It is less often said that no one can succeed in life alone. Less often said, but no less true—or else I wouldn't have a job. Having dedicated my life to helping others achieve their goals—and achieving my own in the process—I have been particularly well placed to notice the effect positive people have on our success. When we surround ourselves with people who not only love us but also believe in us, admire us, and support us through anything, we have the strongest armor for deflecting life's many slings and arrows. What many of us don't appreciate is that we have the power to decide who surrounds us. We ignore this power to our own peril.

A 2006 study looked at the impact that "one bad apple" could have on a group. In the experiment, six groups, each with four members, participated in a series of four twenty-four-minute discussions. One negative person (the "bad apple") was randomly added to one group, whose subsequent behavior and performance as a group was compared to the other three. The "bad apple" did more than simply express negativity and defeatism, but that was certainly among their contributions to the group dynamic. After surveying the results, the study clearly established that the presence of one "bad apple" in a group can have devastating effects on the group, such as decreasing motivation and performance and increasing conflict.

The study looked at only one negative person in a group and the effect this person had over the course of ninety-six minutes. Now imagine having a negative person around you for *years*; imagine the impact this person would have on you. Do you have a negative person in your life? Or several of them? It is time to clean your environment if you want to change your life for the better.

Throughout this book, I have stressed one vital lesson that will help you live in a state of excellence: Develop your confidence so that you can venture into the zone of progress. Until now, I have focused on what you as an individual can do to strengthen your confidence, but I have said little about how others might help you along the way. Yet it is the love, support, and belief of others *in you* that encourages you step out onto the ledge of uncertainty. Like an invisible bridge, the people whom you invite into your life must be able to bear you to the other side. If they can't bear the burden, then you must leave them behind. Your mind is already preprogrammed to accept the negative, to seek comfort and solace, to avoid stepping onto the ledge. You don't need others to reinforce this instinctual trait.

Rather, you need people in your life who can push you further and will never let go. How do you find such people? It's simple: Does this person contribute to your happiness? Does their presence add or subtract from your overall well-being? Does their presence reinforce your self- esteem? Simple in definition, harder in execution. I say that because it is extremely difficult to cut out people who bring us down. We love them, after all. We can still love them even as we choose to venture forward without them. In my own life, I have made the decision to surround myself only with people who believe in me. When I present them with one of my ideas, their first reaction is "How can we make this happen?" It's not "I don't think this is a good idea." It might not be a good idea, but I would rather have those willing to test the idea over those who squash it without further investigation. Likewise, in whatever goal or dream you are pursuing, you need those whose belief *in you* is stronger than the belief you have in yourself. They don't just buy in to whatever goal or dream you are pursuing; they buy into *you*. They believe with all their heart that you can obtain that prize and will turn heaven and earth for you to succeed.

We are all one negative comment away from stepping away from the ledge. Silence the doubters, whether from within or without, embrace the believers, and take that next step into the great unknown.

KEY 9:
Your Entourage Matters

LESSON 1:
Reprogram your inner monologue.
Your inner monologue is programmed to keep you safe and secure. It inundates you, day after day, with negative thoughts that are designed to keep you from taking risks. You cannot silence your inner monologue, but you can reprogram it to start sending you positive messages instead of negative ones. This requires your conscious effort to recognize when and why your inner monologue starts pulling you away from the ledge of uncertainty.

LESSON 2:
Avoid the naysayers.
The people in your life hold a tremendous amount of power over your inner monologue. You are pre-programmed to listen more to those telling you that you can't than those telling you that you can. This is an instinctual trait, and it reinforces your risk-averse inner monologue. A hundred people might be urging you to go forward, but you are programmed to listen to that one person who warns you to go back. Stop spending time with that one person—or any negative person in your life. Reprogramming your inner monologue will count for little if your life is filled with negative people.

LESSON 3:
Develop, nurture, and grow your entourage of believers.

Just as we make a conscious effort to reprogram our inner monologue, so too must we be diligent in deciding who comprises our entourage. Our goal is to fill our lives with people who not only contribute to our overall happiness but also believe in our goals and aspirations. They are not there to shield us from criticism; rather, they are there to hold us up when our own belief falters. Seek out an entourage that will keep you in the progress zone.

TEN

Make Your Motivation

When I became a professional coach, my goal was to have one of my players win a Grand Slam tournament. I announced it to everyone, especially my players. I wanted no one, least of all them, to question where I was going. Every time I fell short, I could feel the expectation I had set taunting me, like a schoolyard bully, as if to say I wasn't good enough to get there. For some, that level of pressure is too much, but I craved it. I thrive under that kind of pressure. I knew what motivated me, and I knew how to generate that motivation. I ran my mouth constantly, ruffling the feathers of those who believed me to be just an upstart—a flash in the pan who would soon fail. Their contempt fueled me as well.

Up until 2012, each of my players made huge jumps in the rankings and got close, but still none had made it. It was like being in a rocket that didn't have quite enough fuel to get into space. We could see the stars, they were tantalizingly near, but then the rocket would fall back to Earth. I would start over and find another player who, like me, needed to prove the doubters wrong. Then it was back to the rocket ship. How close would we get this time? Failure to reach my goal during these early years was difficult for both my players and me (although I learned so much about coaching from every single one of them). Sometimes I was unable to keep a player's motivation high enough to reach the finish line; at other times, the player simply reached their limit. Every professional player does, eventually. It's the rare few whose limits go beyond those of their peers. But I had not reached my limit. Every time I started over, my goal was the same: to win a Grand Slam.

In 2012, within a month of meeting Serena Williams, I reached that goal when she won the Wimbledon title. I had conquered the bully, I had silenced the doubters, I had reached the top of my Everest. Even though I had been her coach for only a short time at this point, she credited me with helping her recover from a first-round loss at Roland-Garros a month earlier. Regardless, Wimbledon was the official start of a collaboration that wouldn't end until 2022. Far from lowering my resolve, winning that first title with Serena only made me want to win more. One of the primary reasons our collaboration was so successful is because we fed off each other's ambitions. It didn't take much to make Serena hungry for another title—a bad tournament, critics in the press, or simply a record to be chased. I'm the same way. The more titles we won, the more I wanted to win. I pushed her when she needed it, and she did the same for me.

Given her age (she was thirty years old when we started), we both knew that the journey wouldn't last forever—eventually the body breaks down, even for the greatest. And yet Serena was playing the best tennis of her life. Every time we crested the top of a mountain—her first French Open win in ten years, the oldest player to be ranked No. 1, the 2015 Australian Open title, breaking Steffi Graf's Grand Slam singles record—we found another one just beyond. Could we reach the top of that one as well?

After that first Wimbledon title, Serena won nine more Grand Slam titles while I was her coach. She won her last one, the Australian Open, in 2017, while pregnant. During our collaboration, she would become the most successful tennis player of the Open Era (the name used to describe professional tennis since 1968). The best there ever was. And yet all things must end.

In 2022, the end came for Serena and me. Something happened that had not happened to me in all my adult years: I lost my motivation. The fire, the drive, the ambition that had propelled me along for more than twenty years had gone out. There were no more mountains to climb. The realization came down on me like a cold rain, and the shadow of depression clouded my mind. I never wanted to coach again.

The Meaning of Motivation

One of the biggest misconceptions about motivation is that it's the juice that gets you up in the morning. Sure, it has that stimulative effect, but caffeine does the same thing. We don't need motivation because we need energy; we need motivation because we need focus and discipline. Can you put in the work that you must *every day until you reach your goal*? In other words, can you perform in a state of excellence at all times?

I'm not here to romanticize hard work for you. When I proposed an intense training and fitness schedule to Aravane Rezai, she broke down in tears. She knew that I was asking her to endure months of grueling work with very little time off. She might have cried, but she accepted. While working with Anastasia (Nastia) Pavlyuchenkova, I instituted very intense practice regimen. She followed along and reached the top thirty in the rankings, but eventually she felt at that very moment the way was too difficult. At the time, she was playing in the world's biggest tournaments and was making excellent money. But to go higher, I needed her to sustain the effort.

She balked. In many ways, she was satisfied with what she had accomplished. She felt she could continue as she was, cruising in her comfort zone, and still compete at the highest levels. She just wasn't prepared to do what she had to do to win a Grand Slam. I told her I was aiming much higher than the top thirty. I was blunt, and I erred in giving her an ultimatum. At the time, I saw her unwillingness as an insult to me. If she wasn't going to work with me, then she was only working against me—against my ambition and my motivation.

It was the wrong attitude for a coach to take. In addition to showing more patience, I should have been looking for solutions to help her rediscover her motivation. Given that Nastia's career continues to this day, and she even reached as high as No. 11 in 2021, she had much more in her than what she showed me at that time. A better coach would have brought it out of her. Looking back now, it's clear that Nastia needed to learn from her experience and mistakes. (So did I.) Plummeting in the rankings has a way of reigniting a player's competitive spirit, as it clearly did for Nastia. Alas, I walked away, my eyes firmly fixed on my goal, fueled by an intense motivation to prove everyone wrong.

> If people don't listen, let adversity teach them.
>
> ETHIOPIAN PROVERB

It might seem odd that I've waited until the final chapter to discuss motivation. Isn't that the *first* thing we need to achieve our goals? In a word, no. The first thing we need is the self-esteem to believe we can achieve our goals, and then we need the confidence to go out and try. I wouldn't say motivation is the last thing we need, only that the foundation you will have built by following the self-coaching keys I have prescribed requires focus and discipline to sustain. And for *that*, you need to be motivated. You need to be locked in on *what matters most*. Because in the end, that's what we're all after—the courage to pursue and the discipline to sustain a course that will bring us joy and make our lives a masterpiece. The goals that accomplish this are different for everyone. But the way we go about achieving them is not so very different at all.

I cannot tell you what motivates you. That's for you to discover, if you don't know already. For fifteen years, from the moment I started my academy with Bob Brett to the moment Serena stepped off the court for the last time, my motivation to succeed in tennis came from the sense that I didn't belong in the sport. I like being the underdog, and it's a common motivation. In any institution or organization, those who have been around the longest tend to act as gatekeepers for the *parvenu*—people like me who threaten their legacy position. My academy, which I deliberately kept separate from the French Tennis Federation, was an upstart, an unwelcome guest. In their own way, they told me to leave. They would spread gossip in the tennis media or whisper to promising young players that my academy was a dead end. They thought they were damaging me. They did the opposite.

The establishment's attempts to stop me only gave me *more* motivation to succeed. The joke was on them the whole time. The more they tried to thwart my goals, the harder I worked to achieve those goals. I demanded to be relevant in the sport I loved. What is a hero to do if he doesn't have a supervillain to stop? That's how I look at it. I actively sought out and encouraged the haters to hate me more. Incidentally, Novak Djokovic is the same. The more the crowd goes against him in a match, the better he plays. Like Djokovic, I need to hear the boos from my detractors to propel me forward. As such, I would say provocative things during press conferences because I knew it would drive them crazy. I also said them because if I put my goals and expectations out there on the public record, I would have to succeed or everyone would see me fall flat on my ass. Believe me, my detractors wouldn't have wasted such an opportunity to gloat. There's some motivation for you.

The point is that I understood what I needed to stay focused on and disciplined in achieving my goals. The boy who never felt like he belonged became the man who never felt like he belonged. The difference between these two versions of me is that the man understood that he didn't have to belong. I had the power to make my own way. It was the lesson I learned as a teenager on that night I told my body to stop vomiting. I had the power. *You* have the power to make your own motivation.

I'm not telling you to go out and make enemies, especially if you're not the sort of person who thrives under tremendous pressure. Serena, like me, needed to put herself on the hook; she said provocative things not simply to annoy her detractors (although that was always fun) but to motivate herself. She said it; now she must do it. She did what she needed to do to stay focused and disciplined. Champions don't wait for motivation; they go out and make it themselves.

What I'm saying is that motivation isn't inspiration. We can be inspired by an event, a person, a book, or a song to do something outside our comfort zone. Because of that, inspiration is a wonderful thing. It's why I stress the importance of having a learning mindset—you never know where and when inspiration will strike. But inspiration happens when we're doing other things. It's not something that's in our power to control. Motivation is. We can't wait for motivation to strike like inspiration because then we will never get started. Often, we must make motivation ourselves.

When I began coaching a new player, one of my first priorities was to learn their motivators. Some players, for example, were motivated when I criticized them. That was the only way I could reach Aravane. It made her feel she was not good enough yet, and I loved watching her wanting more. Others require a softer touch. Serena needed me to fully believe in her while other people challenged and doubted her. When she was motivated, she was like the Hulk: an unstoppable force. For each player, I tailored my approach to their needs. My job was to get the best out of them. To do that, I had to know what made them focus and work through pain and defeat. Once I learned their motivators, I knew I could get them to perform their best.

So you must ask yourself: What will make you work through pain and defeat? Money? Love? Respect? Revenge? It doesn't matter. Motivators don't need to be virtuous to be effective. It's entirely acceptable to admit that you are motivated by the idea of crushing your detractors or proving to those bullies from the playground that they were wrong about you. The only requirement during this self-analysis is that you are honest with yourself. To accept that you can achieve great things from selfish motivations isn't a bad thing. It's simply an acknowledgment that you are human.

Some simple questions to ask yourself include:

When am I performing at my best? The answer should give you insight into the conditions you require to stay motivated.

Is it when you're under a deadline? Is it when you isolate yourself to finish a task? Or perhaps you thrive when surrounded by others? When asking yourself this question, avoid focusing on material things: *If I looked out on the ocean every day, then I could really get some work done. If I could work from home, then I would put in twelve hours a day.* Instead, you must accept your circumstances as they are and try to re-create, as much as possible, the conditions that generate motivation.

Who gains from my success (or failure)? The answer offers a look into what you value most. Are you at your best when others depend on you, like a spouse, children, or friends? Or maybe you are better when you're crushing your enemies and detractors? Again, there are no points for being virtuous and kind in this self-analysis.

How do I handle failure? Look back on the moments when you failed. What was your reaction to the failure? Did you want to crawl into a hole and shut out the world, or was failure just another step for you? We can talk all we want about how we must "use our failures," but I recognize that not everyone is built that way. No number of words from me will change how your truest self handles failure. The only requirement is that you be honest with yourself about it. If failure makes you uncomfortable—if it's debilitating—then your motivation is simple: work so that you *don't fail.*

Just remember that the motivation isn't your goal. We don't strive to live a life of performance excellence because we want to rub it in someone's face. We do it because that's what matters most to us. Motivation is simply a means to an end—and sometimes the means aren't especially virtuous. Accept yours for what they are and proceed to re-create them as often as possible.

The Next Mountain Is Always Taller

The end of my collaboration with Serena didn't happen all in one moment. It was a long process that occurred over several years. In fact, following the birth of her child, I could sense that her main motivation had partly moved away from the court to being a mother. She continued to play for several more years, even reaching four Grand Slam finals, but the reality was that we were both exhausted. I know I was, at least. The past ten years had taken their toll. I wouldn't trade them for anything in the world, but they had left me drained. It was the first time in my coaching career that I had experienced very low motivation, and I needed some time off and a new challenge.

The question of *why* is important for our purposes here. At the beginning of this book, I promised that I would show you how to conquer that first mountain, then conquer all the mountains after. We don't stop when we achieve our goal. Achieving one goal doesn't make us happy. It does for a moment, an hour, a day, a week, but this is not sustainable. What makes us happy is to chase a goal, to put all of our mental focus and energy in the direction of what makes us dream: the journey. And so we move on the next goal, and the one after that.

I had felt drive and determination during my years with Serena. When I saw that our time together was coming to an end, I grew despondent. I had just coached the greatest tennis player of all time; how could I possibly re-create that experience with anyone else? The answer was that I couldn't, and it was this realization that sunk my motivation to coach ever again. I felt that the ride was over and any attempt to re-create it would fail.

When we stop living in the progress zone, we decline. We stop taking chances; we stop seeking out risks. It's only in the progress zone that anything interesting happens. When we stop pushing ourselves, we start to lose our confidence. And when our confidence begins to wane, fear creeps in. In those months after Serena, my mind was clouded with fear. I was afraid I wouldn't find my motivation ever again. I was afraid that I would never reach the heights I had reached with her. My solution was to stop reaching for them at all.

This is a very dangerous moment for us on our journey. When we have achieved all our goals, when we have progressed beyond anything we could have imagined when we first got started on this journey, we can lose our motivation to make that next great effort. But we cannot stop. When we do, then we risk losing all that we have gained to this point. While I don't think that my experience was unique, I was making a fundamental mistake in my thinking. The dream of one day winning a Grand Slam tournament with one of my players had kept me going for eight years before I met Serena. It was all I thought I wanted. I chose potential players based on whether they wanted to win as badly as I did. Some of that judgment was fair, but, as with Nastia, sometimes I let my judgment overrun my coaching. Regardless, sustaining that level of determination—where every day my motivation was a ten out of ten—was grueling.

Then, having achieved that goal, I continued to seek out further challenges, always pushing my goal line farther and farther down the field. I became accustomed to thinking that the only worthy mountains for me to climb were those that *could be climbed only with Serena*. With her, yes, I could strive to break records—but why would that be the only worthwhile goal to achieve? As a coach, why would taking another player to the very top of the sport be any less worthy than what I had done with Serena? Why should it be any less fulfilling? I had been so used to reaching for historic victories that I had forgotten that a coach's job is to get the best performance possible out of a player—whoever that player happens to be. For Serena, her best just happened to be the best of all time. That shouldn't set the standard for other players, nor should it set the standard for my goals as a coach. My goal—my only goal as a coach—is to help my player perform in a state of excellence at all times. When I have done that, I have succeeded. I have climbed the next mountain, which is no shorter than the mountains I climbed with Serena.

I hadn't quite learned this lesson when Simona Halep asked me to coach her in 2022. Rather, I saw a player whose skill had been doubted by the tennis world, a player who had already won two Grand Slams, but who wasn't ready to stop working for the next one, and a player who saw in me a coach who could get her back into contention. I felt my motivation returning. Once I saw the determination in Simona's face, my desire to coach—to return another player to her former dominance—came flooding back. Here was a mountain worthy of climbing!

But the beginning of our collaboration started out badly. In the second round of Roland-Garros, Simona won the first set against Qinwen Zheng 6–2. But she started to panic during the second set, which she lost 2–6. With her composure shattered, she lost the third set 1–6. After the match, she stayed in the physio room, utterly distraught. I hadn't seen the panic attack coming. That told me that I hadn't done my job correctly. I prided myself on always knowing my player's state of mind, but I had missed recognizing Simona's.

I quickly realized why. When we started our collaboration, I noticed that Simona deferred to me in all matters, as if she had no playing style of her own. It was all about what I wanted, and not enough about what she needed. During our practice sessions in the lead-up to the tournament, she would constantly tell me, "I'm not Serena." She would say it apologetically, as if I were comparing her to Serena, which I wasn't. Simona had won two Grand Slam titles without me. She had her own playing style. My focus should have been on learning how to work with her style. But I didn't. I let her respect for me dictate the flow of our practice sessions, in which she did whatever I asked.

The result of all this deferential treatment was that I couldn't identify her emotional cues. One of my greatest strengths as a coach is my ability to read my players. I couldn't with Simona, something I didn't even realize until she suffered a panic attack at Roland-Garros. The moment she faltered, her confidence cratered. She felt that she was letting me down, that she wasn't playing to the level I expected. The panic set in and the rest is history.

That evening, when Simona emerged from her room, I explained all this to her. I accepted the fault for her panic attack on the court. I told her that from then on, my coaching was about her. She didn't have Serena Williams's coach; *I* had Simona Halep as my player. The relationship dynamic had been off from the very beginning, and it was my job to set it to its proper place. When I did, when I tailored my coaching to *her* needs, rather than letting her defer everything to me, we began to function as a team, and I became a coach once more.

One of the critical things I had missed early on was that Simona felt as if she had to perform at the "Serena level." It was too much, and I should have been able to see it tearing her apart. I had believed that by not comparing her to Serena, I was doing enough to dispel those insane expectations. I thought she knew that I just wanted the best *out of her*. But I did not hear what Simona was thinking, which was "I have to perform at the highest level now." After the panic attack, I also understood this. It would change.

What I learned from this experience is that my goal as a

coach from the very beginning wasn't ever about winning a Grand Slam. Believing that this was my goal worked right up to the moment when I lost Serena Williams as a player. Then I had nothing. That's why my motivation vanished. I believed that there weren't any mountains worthy of climbing. And with that realization came depression. I very easily could have given up coaching all together.

It was only when I understood the true nature of my goal that I rediscovered my passion for coaching. It was never about Grand Slams. It was always about helping a player perform at their best. When I achieve that, I climb another, taller mountain. When I am working with a player like that, I am always in the progress zone. I am always challenging myself.

Likewise, when you find yourself losing focus, perhaps even deprived of all motivation, return to what elicited your determination and focus at the beginning. What was it that truly mattered to you? Was it the accolades and success? Unlikely. It was probably something far more personal, something that reduced your passion to its very essence. Return to that feeling. Dust it off. Look at it in a new light, with all the experience you have gained since you first started to reach for it. You will find, as I did, that when you recenter your goals, there is no limit to the motivation that pushes you to achieve them.

Motivation Momentum

One of the beneficial side effects from the end of my collaboration with Serena was that I returned to the business of running the largest tennis academy in Europe. Since becoming a coach, and especially since coaching Serena, I had stepped away from the day-to-day operations of the Mouratoglou

Tennis Academy. It wasn't like I abandoned it, since my work with Serena meant that the academy was swiftly becoming one of the best in the world. But I still left its management and its growth to my colleagues.

In the spring of 2020, while the rest of the world watched anxiously as Covid shut down nearly everything, I was struggling with where to go with Serena. She hadn't officially retired, but it was clear she had slowed down. That left me time for other pursuits. I wasn't interested in coaching anyone else at this time, so I turned my attention to my business. I recognized immediately what Covid meant for us. Not long after the lockdowns started happening, I gathered my team together. For a business that depends on very close, in-person collaboration, the lockdowns posed a serious threat to our success.

"We are in the middle of a major crisis worldwide. We have three options," I told them. "They're the same three options that every business is facing right now. One, we could go out of business. Two, we might stay in business but lose much of our revenue. Or, three, we can get better, open new doors, innovate, and take advantage of the situation. Out of those three options, we're taking the third one."

With that, I turned all my motivation to ensuring that the academy got better while everything around us was getting worse. Perhaps because so much around us was falling apart, I began to look at tennis as an industry. Everyone who works in this sport knows the numbers: Tennis as a sport is in danger for its future. Our average fan is over sixty years old, and getting older every year. We simply aren't reaching enough young people, and there is a very simple reason for this. Tennis, as a form of entertainment, doesn't align with the viewing habits of the young. We can't expect today's kids to watch a two- to three-hour tennis match, with 80 percent of that being downtime, not without some major changes. The younger generations consume media in bite-size pieces—highlights and other short clips that tell the story of a match as if one had watched it live.

With these realities in mind, I posed a question to my team: "If we had to create the sport of tennis *today*, what would we do differently?"

The answers we provided to that question formed the beginnings of the Ultimate Tennis Showdown (UTS) league. Our goal was to provide a version of tennis that was faster, more intense, more entertaining, more authentic. I guess "fast and furious" is a good summary, but a movie studio already coined that phrase. Over the next two months, our team focused on rebuilding the game of tennis from the ground up. In time, we settled on these essential rules::

- Each match comprises four quarters of eight minutes, with simplified scoring (1 point won = 1 point earned).

- The first player to win three quarters wins the match (with a sudden-death round if each player wins two quarters)

- Players get only one serve, and no more than fifteen seconds may pass between points.

Our tournaments would feature only the best players, no more than eight of the highest-ranked players we could get. Our matches would ditch the stuffy and confined etiquette that has dominated tennis for more than a century in favor of a looser, less stodgy environment in which the players and the coaches would be mic'd up and the moments between points filled with high-velocity music.

To say that UTS was an ambitious attempt is an understatement. Once more, the gatekeepers of the tennis world said I would fail. They said UTS would only demean the integrity of the sport and turn off our audience. Good. I was the underdog once more. I used the naysayers as motivation to put all my determination and focus into making UTS a reality. I went one step further and announced that our first tournament would be held in eight weeks. My staff could have killed me, but I knew that it was the best way to motivate them. At least it was for me. I threw myself into ensuring that UTS would be a success. I called the players we wanted to invite; I made the pitches to investors; I negotiated with TV channels for coverage; I haggled with the stadiums where we wanted to hold our tournaments. In just a few weeks, I had become an entrepreneur again, something I had not done since I first started my academy.

We held the first two tournaments at the academy, where we televised the matches all over the world. It was a necessary consolation given the eight-week deadline I had imposed, but it all worked. It also led to larger venues and more investors. In July 2023, our tournament in Los Angeles, at the Dignity Health Sports Park, sold out. Our second event, in Frankfurt a few months later at the Süwag Energie Arena, also sold out. With the naysayers silenced, a new tennis league had been born. We had created a form of tennis that could not only exist but thrive alongside the traditional leagues. My challenge to my team in the spring of 2020—to ensure that our business got better—proved successful. They had answered the call and created something at a time when so much was being destroyed. In 2024, we played in Oslo, New York, Frankfurt, and London.

And that provides us with the final lesson on motivation: At a time when my motivation to coach had all but disappeared, I found a new source to keep me in the progress zone. Motivation, like momentum, is easier to create when you're already moving. When you stop, when you revert to the comfort zone, you're only making it that much harder to find the motivation to start it all up again. You cannot stop. When one source of motivation closes for you, you must actively seek out another. To remain motionless is to give up all you have achieved along your journey thus far. Always keep moving.

After Serena, it would have been the easiest thing in the world for me to stop. Part of me wanted to. After all, my record as a coach would have been unassailable. I had the titles to prove that I had achieved all the goals I had set for myself. What was left for me to do? No one would have faulted me for taking a step back.

Except I had learned the most important lesson from a journey that had begun forty years earlier when I was a scared, sickly child who couldn't talk to anyone: We don't embark on a journey to reach the end. There is no end. We embark on a journey because it will help us become the best version of ourselves. We start moving forward because to stand still is to deny ourselves life's greatest gift: that we are meant to reach our fullest potential. When we endeavor to live a life of performance excellence, we are accepting the challenge to make our lives a masterpiece.

KEY 10:
Make Your Motivation

LESSON 1:
Motivation isn't inspiration.
You don't need motivation because you struggle to find the energy to work toward your goals. You need motivation because it gives you the power to bring the focus and determination that is required to achieve your goals. Anything worth achieving requires hard work, and pain and tedium are the price you pay to reach your goals. To work through that pain and tedium, you must find your motivation.

LESSON 2:
You have the power to create the motivation you need.
If you wait for motivation to arrive, you will be waiting for a long time. Instead, you must understand when and how you perform at your best and re-create those conditions consistently. What motivates you doesn't need to be virtuous or pure; it simply needs to make you do the work that is required.

LESSON 3:
Motivation keeps you moving.
When you lose your motivation, you stop moving. You stop living in the progress zone and once more live a life ruled by fear and doubt. To maintain your confidence, you must always be looking for new avenues for motivation. Only with the proper motivation will you continue to live in the progress zone.

CONCLUSION:

Follow the Game Plan

My message to my players before they walk onto the court is the same regardless of the player or opponent: follow the game plan. If they follow the game plan, they will win. I have a slightly modified message for you as you prepare to step out onto the court of your life. If you follow the game plan as I presented it in this book, you will win—even if you lose.

What do I mean by that? Just this: All we can control in life are our own actions. The way we control our actions is with the proper mindset. When we master our minds, our bodies—or actions—will follow. We will then be performing in a state of excellence. We continue to do so even if, when we follow the plan perfectly and achieve every one of our goals, we somehow lose. The way I would define "losing" in this case is that the object of our effort escapes our grasp.

That's life. We don't always get what we want.

I'm not trying to prepare you for disappointment. Instead, I want you to look at what it means to win in a different way. As much as I have used the metaphor of the tennis match to illuminate my lessons, you are not, in the end, playing on a court with an opponent. Your court is your life, in whatever way you choose to define it. Perhaps you have a real opponent, someone who is consciously working against you. But for most things in life, this isn't the case. For all of us, the opponent we are trying to defeat *every day* is ourselves. We pursue the keys set forth in this book to overcome the many ways in which our minds work against us. And no matter how many times we might win this battle with ourselves, each day is a new fight. But it does get easier. More importantly, your desire to win this fight every day only gets stronger. You will, as I do, awake each day ready to fight and ready to win.

That's what I mean about winning: We keep that uncertain, powerless boy or girl inside us at bay for another day; the one that lacks confidence, the one that is terrified of leaving their comfort zone; the one that stays uncurious about the world and pays too much attention to their inner voice telling them that to take risks is too dangerous. We live in the progress zone where we push our limits, expand our knowledge, and achieve our goals. We remain, in short, in a virtuous cycle, where the only loss that truly matters is the one that takes us out of it. Every day that we stay in a virtuous cycle, we have won.

Because even if the prize or dream remains out of reach, you have moved forward. You have progressed. We *change* in the progress zone; we must or we won't last long. We don't stay the same person. Every day we become a little bit more of a champion.

If you follow the plan, *this will happen. You will win.*

But I repeat what I said at the start of this book, it will take time. First, we don't try to do too much too soon, but we do something every day. As I do with my players, you must lower your criteria for what constitutes a victory. Embrace the ethos of "little victories" each day. *Get used to winning.* Build that foundation of self-esteem and confidence and find moments to act outside your comfort zone. Don't overthink it.

But whatever you do, *act*. One step forward today is more than you did yesterday.

Second, be kind to yourself. To overhaul your present mindset into a champion mindset will force you to confront your own weaknesses in ways you've never imagined. Most of us avoid our weaknesses or ignore them. We get through life by imagining they're not there. Yet, to follow the plan means that sometimes our weaknesses and fears get the best of us. Don't stop. This is an uncomfortable process, and you must be able to forgive yourself if you don't fully succeed at first. But here is where I stress again that we don't succeed in life alone. The people in your life are there because they are your biggest supporters. Share with them your dream. They will want you to succeed and help you along your journey. They will look on you with kind eyes just as you must.

All of us are on our own Grand Slam journey. We're all striving for something that seems out of our reach and beyond our talents. But we strive for it nevertheless, because it produces our best self. You will stumble, as I did, but you will find it in yourself to get back up. You will know victory at the end of one journey, only to realize that you are ready to start another. Through this process, you will find peace and happiness. You will begin living your one life as a masterpiece, with no single victory or defeat defining your destiny, and become the person you were always meant to be.

ACKNOWLEDGMENTS